A Poetry Anthology
Inspired by Horror

DARK INK

a poetry anthology
inspired by horror

MOON
TIDE PRESS

~2018~

Dark Ink: A Poetry Anthology Inspired by Horror

Editor-in-chief
Eric Morago

Associate Editor
Michael Miller

Marketing Specialist
Ellen Webre

Proofreader
Jim Hoggatt

Front cover art
Leslie White

Back cover & title page art
Tyler Kinnaman

Book design
Michael Wada

Moon Tide logo design
Abraham Gomez

Dark Ink: A Poetry Anthology Inspired by Horror
is published by Moon Tide Press

Moon Tide Press #166
6745 Washington Ave. Whittier, CA 90601
www.moontidepress.com

FIRST EDITION

Printed in the United States of America

ISBN # 978-0-9974837-6-5

CONTENTS

FOREWORD

If fear cannot be articulated, it can't be conquered.

—Stephen King, *Salem's Lot*

I was *that* kid who made their parents promise there were no monsters before saying goodnight, who (not taking any chances) would check that the closet door was shut tight (sometimes more than once), and would, on occasion, ask for the hall light to remain on until I fell asleep. But, I was also a kid who was completely fascinated by that which I feared would snatch me away each night.

Every time my dad would take me with him to the local video rental store, I would sneak off to the horror section. I'd study the gory box art of those VHS cassette tapes as if I were at a museum—as if I knew I was looking at something I did not yet understand, but wanted to. Eventually, imagining monsters did not impede my sleep, the closet door was left ajar, and I didn't mind the dark.

I don't remember the first horror film I actually saw because, once I stopped being scared, I became so obsessed I binge-watched as many I could rent one summer. I can't recall if it was *Nightmare on Elm Street* or *Poltergeist* that I first popped into the VCR and watched on that 13-inch television in my bedroom. Maybe it was the *Omen*? I do vividly recount my eleven-year-old eyes affixed to the screen when Damien's nanny leaps off the balcony and hangs herself during his birthday party, exclaiming, "It's all for you, Damien." I thought: *This is some crazy shit!*

As I grew older, I began to appreciate the complexities of the horror genre—how monsters were metaphors and the stories surrounding them commentary on our own society or psychology. This is one of the things that also attracts me to poetry. A poem's straightforward narrative can imply multiple layers of meaning; the success of this merely rests on the intent and skill of the poet.

Horror is somewhat of a niche within film; it can often be overlooked as not having the same artistic merit as other works within the medium. The same too can be said, I'm sure, of poetry that chooses to celebrate horror within its lines and stanzas. However, I've always been an advocate for more pop culture in today's poetry, because of that word *popular*—I want the poems I read and write to attract, be understood, and enjoyed by a *larger* audience. I believe that can be achieved by placing the occasional zombie in a poem, so long as the poet doesn't sacrifice substance for shtick.

In this anthology, you will find well-crafted poems that play with, deconstruct, poke fun at, pay homage, and respond to, not only horror films, but also literature, folklore, mythology, and monsters—the entire scope of horror and its tropes. Anything that goes bump in the night is fair game. Why? Because there is something truly intoxicating about fear. There is a reason why so many people read and watch things that scare them. It's an escape—how the heart races when we know something horrible is coming, muscles tightening as the suspense builds, the fighting with ourselves to both look and turn away.

But worry not—if you are a timid reader, this collection is not meant to scare you; these are not "scary" poems. The 66 poets who appear in this book are, like myself, writers who simply see the worth and wonder of horror, and explore that in their poetry. Though, if you share our same fascination with fearful subject matter, reader, you will feel quite at home. We've left no gravestone unturned. *Dark Ink: A Poetry Anthology Inspired by Horror* has something for everyone to enjoy—those who still check their closet doors each night, those who do not, and those who leave them purposely wide open, as if inviting something in.

Eric Morago
Publisher
Moon Tide Press

Robin Axworthy

GOBLIN'S ESCAPE

This mistake is a goblin let loose. Just a small one,
but he's escaped through a gap in the door.

He runs about and grimaces and pinches
and lets the world know he's mine.

He joins the others freed on this day or another,
that time or sometime, recently or long ago,

all bearing news of my mistakes, while crowds of others
inside chitter and dance, waiting for their chance—

the next time I forget and leave the side door open,
or a window unlatched. Such simple mistakes, really.

I long to rope them in, hide them from you, hope
you will not notice them mocking me behind my eyes,

dancing round my skirt, bang-banging on my heart,
and chanting *nah-nee-nah-nee* so I don't even hear you

when you say: *it doesn't matter in the least, my love,
this mistake.*

MEDUSA'S MANIFESTO

I would sit and gaze at the open sea—
the glassy rocks, the wine-red waves
glanced with sun. I watched as ships
with their ranks of oars and sails
woven on a loom by women like me
carried my brothers away in search of glory,
battle, slaves, or gold to carry home.

O gods, how I longed for that air, that sea.
But you made me a woman. Why would I *not*
curse you? I was wound in the fine white linen
of my caste and my face was my father's to give
away, or not, on whom he chose. My only weapon?
Seduction, that sly dissimulation women learn
to use in halls where brothers, fathers, husbands,
drink themselves asleep on the mead *we* women
carry. They stuff themselves on meat *we* butchered,
cleaned, and roasted—on the bread *we baked*—
while the bards sing of wars, of heroes, and
the immortality of a name. There, they drank
and wept and called for more and I hated
all of them.

But then, Athena, jealous goddess, freed me.
No man to serve or carry for. Now I stand
on rocks, looking out over the sea, where spittle-
foamed waves leap up to meet the heavy sky.
My bright hair—a regal crown of snakes.
My power is my own, and any man who sets
to master me, or win fame by conquest?
Instant death. I earned *this*. This prize—
this curse—my name and story sung by bard
and harp in warriors' halls. Yet in the end
it seems I am still a slave to the gods,
still assailed by men, still held by rock
and shore. Never to have my face
set high among the stars, so below

mothers, holding their daughters,
could point and say, *Look, there,*
my dearest one, is the great Medusa.

Devon Balwit

CAGEY

The ship has been programmed to self-destruct. The corridors blare and strobe with panic. The only survivor, you rush to the landing craft, the whoosh of the airlock echoing your relief. Small engines thrust you seconds ahead of detonation. The red flare that follows should have sufficed to kill your nemesis, but verb tense is everything. The alien has been one step ahead of you this whole time. Now you share a single placental sac. Even naked, you must be lethal. When the hatch opens, only one of you must emerge.

WOMB

The skeleton's ribs have been blasted open from inside. One of us suggests leaving, but we don't. How would our race advance if we ran away from violations of bodily integrity? Instead we intrude into the alien nursery, allow the ovipositor deep into our throats. We know what grows within us will kill us, but not before we are pregnant with the unknown.

Laurel Ann Bogen

ALSO FRANKENSTEIN

Because he was mine the thing I made screamed
when he felt the light…

—Lawrence Raab

Behemoth, I called him
he, too, was mine
clumsy and large
oddly endearing.
He wanted so to please me
brought me crystal and tissue.
It was all the same to him
gifts from the Magi
or coffee filters.

I wanted more
from my own creation—
was that wrong?
I wanted the stellar
and black cosmos
I wanted illusion
I wanted—
dare I say it—
devotion…

Certainly he was devoted
he had no choice.
I filled his hours
with marvels of my humanity
his rooms with my grandiose longing.

But he wasn't content
with my mythology
my reasoning.
The folly of Icarus
flew before me.

Still I gave in.
I opened the thin edge
of the wedge,
stood before him
trembling and radiant.
I reached inside my chest
here is where it burns
and *here*
and *here...*

My thin hands
held that cold pale light.
It glittered with a blue flame
and flecked with ice.

BONES DIG THIS DREAM

she knew it
couldn't explain it
followed her great
yearning for bones
tibia
femur
phalange
cut her teeth
on bones
bones dig grave
thirteenth hour yips
dead leaves at her feet

marrow root she hisses
more than skin
she digs deeper
kneads and massages
until she feels bone
     NOW
O Grave Undertaker
root of this dream
be bone
be marrow
be what you mean.

OCTOBER KNOB AND BROOM

I.

Wind holds as the bonfires
grow crackle and spark.
Maple leaves fly away crows
caw and caw—
what witness do you bear
jackdaw and superstition?

All Hallows' Eve
and my rusted hobgoblins
so many apples bobbing on icy waters
rise up shiver and haunt.

Children bloated and sweet
grin like fat little pumpkins
of summer-made flesh
predict gifts under a sharp and radiant moon.

As I needle and crochet shawls
from my jagged bones,
rattle cast and spin—
tooth of the earth

And winter is a-coming soon...

II.

(What do you fear?)

Amanda J. Bradley

QUEEN KONG

*Where is the ebullient, infinite woman who…hasn't been ashamed of
her strength? Who, surprised and horrified by the fantastic tumult of her
drives…hasn't accused herself of being a monster?*

> —Héléne Cixous, "The Laugh of the Medusa"
> (Translated by Keith Cohen and Paula Cohen)

I've been shimmying up skyscrapers all my life,
swatting at airplanes that buzz by my massive head.
I have been holding tiny men in my palm, careful
not to squish life from their fragile bodies.
I have spent my rage on the bars of this cage. Ripped
from my native habitat, I can barely remember
I am not a monster. My drives are ancient and furious.
I peer into the tiny windows of your offices
and see you skitter about in monkey suits.
You think you are making the world go round,
mastering complex transactions, but the world
is simpler than that. It is the stench of my breath
roaring at you through fangs clenched in a wide,
diabolical smile, showering shattered glass at your feet.

VILLAIN

It was my favorite cartoon, but *Scooby Doo* gave me nightmares.
Did I not understand when the mummy costume came off
in the end it was just a criminal underneath?
Or is that precisely what I understood? Why should it be a relief
that someone would pretend to be a ghost to steal money?

Most people don't think of themselves as bad people, a friend suggested.
This makes all the finger pointing we do in society seem peculiar.
We all have our pet laws we are willing to break: speeding and pot smoking
for some, wife beating and armed robbery for others. Even the serial killer
sees himself, above it all, as pure. *What is evil*, he might wonder.

Why do bad things happen to good people, we ask.
Where does evil come from? In part, from not seeing ourselves
as bad people. I have done many things to forgive myself for.
I hope my recognition helps me tip the scales for the world.
I hope when my mask comes off, I am not a villain.

Derek D. Brown

BLACK MAGIC

As a Black man,
I was born going bump in the night.
Never cast as a friendly ghost,
but rather an unholy spirit,
labeled "spook."

I was the original boogey-man,
but ankle shackles made it hard to dance.
They tried to silence my song and bound my rhythm in chains,
but my mere presence is the reason all the other monsters mash.

In nature,
the darkest soil bears the most fruit.
But the only thing that seems to grow from my onyx complexion
is the size of the bullseye on its sable hue.
They're scared of the way it thrives in the blaze of the sun,
yet still bays loudly at the full of the moon.

Walking midnight,
manifested as man.
With all this voodoo I'm wrapped in
it's no wonder I'm branded as curse.
You can try and chase me out of town
with a torch and a pitchfork,
but we all know
who lived here first.

Cathleen Calbert

AT DUSK

The Vampire Lady does a languorous striptease before seven full-length mirrors that stand as sentries around her otherwise unused "living room." As she does so, she sings: *Feet long boats, ankles a deer's, calves a girl's, hips a shipwreck, waist a drawing in of breath, neck a dying swan's face* . . . Here the Lady V. never knows which lyrics fit. Her face is beautiful, horrible, young, and old the way ladies' countenances can be in Hollywood, as smug as the mugs of Renaissance Madonnas, la Gioconda, and Medusa, weary as Parisian absinthe drinkers or Thai ladyboys, masculine underneath its femininity, below the lilac eye shadow and the dark lips, Weimar sexy, Upper East Side cool, an alluring, captivating, skin-tingling nothingness. *Forever,* the Lady sings and turns to whatever lover is or isn't there.

EXAM ROOM

The Vampire Lady goes to the doctor, who says she's anemic. *Oh, that can't be true*, she murmurs; he prescribes liver and onions nonetheless. *Surely, a shot of Jameson in the afternoon will do*, she whispers, but he shakes a bottle of pills that are black and thick as licorice. *More red meat*, she offers him. *And hopelessly pessimistic*, he says. *The state of the world*, she shrugs. He says that she must have a winning attitude in order to be one of life's winners. Her bad attitude might lead to bad things for her, even to the loss of certain lady parts. By the end of this dressing down, the Lady V. is a slumped girl in a paper gown. She's a plucked goose, a doomed pullet, a sucker. After donning her Christian Dior and repainting her lips, she knuckles her doctor down to the examination table, where she draws forth cat-claws of his blood. *What a pain*, the Vampire Lady says as the man faints to the floor. Once again, she needs a new physician.

Michael Cantin

FROM THE DARK WOODS A BANJO PLAYS

1.
This here story,
it's as true as seasons,
as dangerous as torch light,
as nasty as old scratch himself.
You know it to be true,
don't you doubt me, boy.
You won't doubt them gators
when they flee a heart
as cold and reptilian
as their own.

2
Draw near faerie fire:
lead the lost ones to their homes.
Burn live the sinner.

Tempo soft for believer,
shrill chords to mark damnation.

3.
Don't look back.
Don't look. Back.
Don't. Look back.
Don't.
Look.
Back.

4.
Sunday school teaches
be afraid,
just as churches teach
to condemn.

There is music at the crossroads.

Adrian Ernesto Cepeda

WOULD GODZILLA DATE ME?

Forget Jim Morrison,
my sister loves this Lizard
King. Trying to reason
with her crush, I explain
Godzilla will always leave
you to paint the town fire-
breathing red. This anti-hero,
never sleeps, he prefers NYC
to Hollywood, and igniting
cigarettes blazes in warehouse
clubs to the tallest starlets
with the smokiest breaths.
Her future boyfriend
would have the biggest
temper, he'd rather blow
the roof with his trademark
steam, giving the fans
trademarked explosive tantrums
from the silver screen.
What happens when cable
networks ignore this giant
because this beast's destruction
symphony already sounds
like scroll news? So, Godzilla
makes unannounced appearances
attacking Tokyo, Frisco waiting
for the cameras to reclaim
his wrinkling name, picturing
future headlines: all this fame
has gone way over his dragon-
head. What happens when TMZ
cameras stop flashing and he resorts
to hanging underneath the Brooklyn
bridge, relighting blunts with hipster
potheads? *Would Godzilla date
me?* She cries in the middle

of night. *I could change*
him, rewrite the ending
remaking his...a modern-
day tail, a happy, fairy
one is what she declares,
while cuddling with her
stuffed-animal monster
dreaming of the night
her massive beau
bends down on his gigantic
corpse-stained knees.
For all the ones who
couldn't stand his heated
temper, she mumbles:
they deserved it under
her breath, she'll convince
herself: *My 'zilla*
would never hurt me.
So, misled, my sister waits
her own flame, pining skyward
towards his gargantuan
poster towering over her
searing bedsheets.

Sarah ChristianScher

OBLIGATORY FRANKENSTEIN POEM

He used to stubbornly ignore it,
when they called him the wrong name.
On the street.
In Starbucks.
Not my name, he says in his head every time.
Not what is chosen, but what was given
and left
like he gave life but not the knowledge of living;
learned it from the slap of many palms,
hiss of match,
and snap of kindling.
He wonders if he feared the mirror of fire;
stiff limbs given life, made to burn.

Now he just gives in.
They call him Frankenstein;
he doesn't fight it anymore.
Thinks he hears his father laughing,
bitterly in his ears every time.
Every time he thinks he becomes more
like his own monster
with each name they take from him.

SIREN

(noun)
1. a device that makes a loud prolonged sound as a signal or warning.
2. In Greek Mythology, each of a number of women or winged creatures
whose singing lured unwary sailors onto rocks.

—*Webster's Dictionary*

Someone once told me
I had a voice made for love songs,
back when I spent my nights searching for a hero.
Brave captains and bold ship-hands,
Their skin like salt and their stubble like sand.
But men of the sea have barnacle-encrusted hearts,
So I gave up on my bonny sailor boy;
moved inland to smokey clubs and lounges,
still singing for my supper.

Baby, come here.
I won't lie to you,
I don't remember my lovers' names.
Not even the one who dropped,
limp and lifeless from the warmth of my embrace,
as I opened my arms
to welcome you home.

Baby, come here.
Pay no mind to the lovers I've abandoned.
Legions of them.
Broken sea shells.
Empty husks on a desolate stretch of beach.

Baby, come here.
Things will be different this time,
trust me.

THE WITCH'S ADVICE

I've given you a choice—
one that I made,
long ago when my skin was eggshell smooth
and limbs straight as my broom handle.
Before this twisted body and leathery flesh,
my brother sat in *that* cage
looked out with pleading eyes,
mouth all a tremble,
as the sound of the witch sharpening her knives
and the crackling firelight
whispered secrets,
murmured that I could free only one.
The choice was mine to make
neither my brother nor the witch could see;
they were too close to it,
lost in a forest of trees.
But I could pull back,
create distance
find the way out.
The knife or the fire.
Put one to my brother,
or the witch in the other.
Blood is thicker than water,
but stew spiced with betrayal has more flavor.
Witches are free to do as they please,
and if I'm honest with you, Gretel:
you aren't pretty enough for your own story.

Nicole Connolly

HOW YOU MADE THE MOST OF WEAK FIRE MAGIC

We locked ourselves in your bedroom,
away from your stepfather. One by one, you lit matches
against the side of their box and stared at them
until they fizzled harmless to smoke, always before touching
your fingers. I sat on the floor and tried to hold your pug still;
she'd scratch me and run circles around the bed. They say dogs are sensitive
to ghosts, so must they be to magic. *It works*, you said,
when you tell each flame that it deserves to die, over and over
until it does. You graduated to candles—tea lights,
then ones long and drippy; finally, wide wax in a jar.

You hadn't learned how to convince something to live,
so you could never set anything alight. If you could, you would
have heated the wrench in your stepfather's hand
when he chased you to the car and beat on the windshield;
you would have branded him. At family functions, you gathered
cousins to tell scary stories at the fireplace,
raised and lowered its colors like a curtain for effect.
I was the only one who knew this was you,

and at the beach, you ruled the bonfire, when everyone
was drunk on Kraken rum snuck into cans of Dr. Pepper,
they didn't notice that when the blaze dimmed, you stared at me,
grinned when they left to steal more palm fronds
from the community compost. We stood alone
on opposite sides of the pit, suddenly a bed of coals so cold
we could have held each other in the center of them. And you,
tiger-striped orange and black in their reflection, looked beautiful
for the first time. You thought about all the reasons to die
with more intensity than ever before, and we kissed
over the pit, your upper lip brief between my own.
When the first new frond fell in, you released
your hold, erupted a tower that singed
the tips of our hair. Everyone screamed,
and you boiled over, laughed like he'd never

pushed you down a flight of stairs on your way
to eat dinner. I think you realized, for the first time,
you weren't the only person who could be afraid,
because the next morning, after her night shift,
your mother returned to her blackened-skeleton home,
found you huddled, pug held in your scratched arms
and still trying to scramble away, your skin gray-striped,
while you stared at a corpse fallen from the master bedroom
into the kitchen, with not enough evidence left to find out
it was you who had pushed a dresser against his door
while he napped. *A freak electrical fire*, they said,
and no way, it seemed, you couldn't be dead. *A miracle*,
they said; someone's god must have held you then
in his endless, invisible arms.

SELF-PORTRAIT AS EXACTLY THE KIND OF MONSTER MEN'S RIGHTS ACTIVISTS WARN EACH OTHER I AM

In the online character generator, I build the body I want to be me—
scaly, gigantic, gut meter slid all the way to the right, skull angular

until wholly unappealing, six piercings along the bridge of my slitted
nose. I suppose I look tough because even though I'm very, remarkably bad

at this game, strangers want to fight alongside me and my oddly-shaped
sword and my oddly-shaped head and my full-body armor with a cut-out

for my tail—which is not a cutesy tail—which is not a cat tail from
a bargain-bin anime or a fox tail on the end of a Pornhub buttplug—

a tail that is wholly larger than the whole span of the average man
who plays this game. The first time I tried to build a body in a massively

multiplayer online computer world, my friend came over after
a sweaty day of sweaty, middle school boys trying to grab our titties

to show me her preferred universe, where life science class amounted to
slashing open monsters until many red pixels of blood erupted.

Out of two body options, I chose the one most like me—breasty
and clad in standard-issue starter rags—and fumbled out of the tutorial

into the chat of a strange man who said he would give me a new shirt
if I got on my knees and cybered with him. At thirteen, and terrified,

and with strict parents, so strict I had barely been initiated into PG-13 movies,
I didn't know what cybering—or a blow job—was but understood my knees

had—somehow—taken on a significantly terrifying new significance,
and my terrified friend grabbed the sweaty keyboard with her sweaty

hands and made my avatar with her dagger of merely five, pebble-colored
pixels run away. And somewhen in-between these two body-

building occurrences, I had to sneak someone out of an apartment
complex through the fire escape with a stun gun and pepper spray,

and some unrelated dude some unrelated day screamed at me
from the upper deck of a train, asking if I get off on being such

a bitch—no, I do not get off on being the mediocre bitch of every sadboy's
dystopia—how much easier it would be to just exist as a seven-feet tall,

anthropomorphic crocodile. How many talking alligator lizards must
I do a mystical favor for to be granted the monstrous body of my dreams?

How many interdimensional reptile gods would I have to invoke
with a brine-soaked spellbook? Next time a strange man takes off

the bikini top of another strange woman in the water, I want to be
hidden at the bottom of that lake. I want to take each testicle in

my mouth until many red splooshes of blood whorl out, then carry them
between my yellow-plaque teeth, gentle as though they are hatchlings.

SELF-PORTRAIT AS FIRST SLUT TO DIE IN A HORROR MOVIE

I manifest in lingerie, red as a cursed midnight. Compare me
to the moon—not for my beauty, for the way I make wolves.

The lover's body: a Ouija board. They tell me I asked for this
devil, otherwise lurking on the other side of a gauzy veil—

yet, the worst haunt is myself. My own ghost breathes into me
like a phone bell, from somewhere inside this rib-lined house. I try

to love someone and watch myself die. *Why flee to the woods?*
They are indistinguishable—hockey-mask man, man undressed.

*How could you run so barefoot? Crawl away with your thigh
sliced open as a gusty window?* I have practiced feeling this

nothing. It's cursed magic, the way I could lie still as a corpse
under his hand. They tell me I have lived my life by the wound;

my body justifies the hatchet. How the film won't work unless
I didn't want most of it to happen to me—only just enough.

SELF-PORTRAIT AS MANIC
EXTRATERRESTRIAL DREAM GIRL

If this were not a science-fiction movie,
the story would begin here: at the grocery store,
where you put the receipt in my hand
and touched my fingers a little too long.

It would begin if, when you small-talked
and told me how much you didn't like the latest
blockbuster movie, I had listened to
the translator planted in my sternum. It told
me to say, *would you like the movie more
if you saw it a second time, with me?*

I didn't say it. I see, still, in your eyes,
the closest a human being can get
to time travel. I see you imagine me,
already waking up alongside you in bed.

Because this is a science fiction movie,
if I had said the words, the story would begin
not really in the grocery store, but when
I have to tell you that I am an alien, maybe
someone you have wanted to rescue you
from Earth all this time—and it is true
that I can go so, so high, until nothing
of this world can touch me. I can't say

the words knowing how all these movies
end. Once you see the first spaceship on screen,
the viewer knows there's little chance here
for everlasting love; it's not in the genre. I time travel

in the human way, too, see us looking
at the sky. You are angry, because you see me
long for stars I left behind, and that's not
even what I'm doing. I am trying to point out
planets too far away for you to see. Eventually,

you will want me to look at you and think
of nothing else I've known, but I've known
so much more than you understand.
Eventually, you'll want to give me a diamond,
maybe a handful, but do you know there are
planets where diamonds are all it rains?
I could go—You don't have the lungs for it.

You'd dislike me for being presumptuous,
though I know this could only end one way:
the human, looking up at my escape craft,
not being able to see if the alien is looking
back. Do you want to know now if I would?

Yes, though only for as long as I can
see your hand wave—not long.

Scott Noon Creley

CTHONIC (AN ELDRITCH LOVE STORY)
for HP Lovecraft

*Really the hardest part about being a gibbering, squamous prophet of the old ones isn't
the saintly hunters, or competing gods, or the nameless horrors who will eventually awake
and consume you despite your unholy devotion—it's the dating scene. It breaks you.*

   —Nyarlthotep, the Crawling Chaos

Don't look at me like that;
I don't like the pity in your uncountable dull eyes.
And don't whisper those usual
cobwebbed and snapping bits of dark prophecy,
those same never-written prayers.

Yes, I've tried all the websites—
Gnashr, Dead but Dreaming (of Love), Farmers Only.
None of them work. All people want are infinitely refracting selfies
where my true twisted nature is laid bare to the world.
All they want to do is ogle me and send their friends into gibbering
peals of maddened laughter and ragged warlock prayers.
Also, the farmers popped like rotten grapes, and that wasn't great.

Is there anything out there in the vast, flickering catacomb of the universe?
Is there an endless screaming hymn for a terror priest like me?
Must I be forced to witness every yowling and cavorting goat-faced beastman
as he courts some achingly thin phosphorescent ghoul?
Must I lament as they stride across the Miskatonic campus
plucking souls and flicker-flashing between the shadows
as if they invented it? As if their great endsong were the first?

No, don't suggest that.
No, I'm done with those places.
They're accursed flesh markets.
They make me feel like a slab of rubbery meat,
as if I were just bloated, writhing tentacles—
like my only value is my hideous, inverted biology,
my sticky heaving vexed reality.
I can't stand that. I'm more than that.
I'm endless, really.

Besides, the prices in the *Mountains of Madness* are outrageous.
I can't just throw away a few centuries and a handful of cultists
every time I want a sip of dying antiquarian starlight.
I don't want to just stare at the singular creatures from across the bar,
to spend all night chatting up the inky storm of a cavorting shoggoth,
who has soaked his fetid flanks in far too much poisonous moon water,
so that the whole bar shimmers with the lavender hues of his unknowable madness,
the way heat bends light in the desert.

I can't bear to pay the cover at *Pickman's Catacombs*. Again.
I'll end up having to slouch home past some screaming occult scholar
as he weeps into a dead radio for help,
as if he hasn't already passed the edge of it all,
as if he isn't so far past the silver gates
that tomorrow he'll never have even existed.

What's that?
No, I don't feel sorry for the humans. They're nosey.
It's just that sometimes I feel the same way.
That I'm fragile. That I might be smaller than I thought.
That someday I'll be as isolated as old Cthulhu,
waiting for those strange aeons where even death might die.

I just don't want to go home to my tomb—
it always feels so cyclopean, empty, unhallowed.
So suddenly Euclidean and mundane.
A place filled not with apocalypses, or creeping colors out of space,
just a room with a rickety table, a candle, an open tome
reeking of the ordinary misery.

It's all too bourgeoisie. Too gauche. I can't even be bothered
to rally the cultists. To rearrange the stars or spout squamous prophecy.
I don't even want to lead the unholy procession
through the crumbling pyramids of Nth.

No, I know. I know. It's fine. I'm fine.
I just need to find some new madness,
to twist myself into some new, terrible shape,
to black out the heavens like a snuffed match,
to crack the firmament like stale communion
in the hands of a defiled nun.
Or maybe take up needlepoint and stay in.

Thanks, mom. I know.
R'yleh P'tagahn Yr.
I love you too.
To the audient void and back again.

THE FAITH HEALER

I.
She hates to feel the wounds
knitting back together, pulsing
under her hands, thin threads of flesh
writhing invisibly across the pink divide.
This is the secret palette of wounds, of cataracts,
the whistling echoes in puncture wounds,
the feeling of eyes made glassy then cloudy again.

II.
In the field, she found a dead rabbit,
white and black, his flanks gold with dust.
She touched the nape of its neck,
let its cold, dead thoughts
flicker up her fingertips,
let them dissolve
in the black flame she keeps inside—
there, then gone,
slow as ice in a hot mouth.

The rabbit's back legs twitched, its slitted eyes
opening wide, wider, its mouth working
in the still wet morning air
as if it had found words,
but could not shape them.

She watched as its tiny claws scratched pictograms
in the bluish earth between the shadows of the stalks.

She tried to decipher what it all might mean—
what unmaking scripture might sit at the center of the nothing.

III.
She, of course, has to bring the wounds back.

Nobody has ever told her,
but there is an equation to this world, a balance.
That, as her teacher has inscribed in slate and chalk,
an expression must be made even.

Cancer feels the worst as it returns,
when it blossoms back out again
in slow twitching heaves, black ink
through black water
and fills her with shaking, sweating venom.

That moment reminds her
that we are all colorless inside, without witness
until we are open and under the knife.
That our blessings and curses are all irreversible,
the words of them already long spoken—

that each life is really just thread
dangling loose and ragged
in the eye of the mortician's needle,
that we are all just a stitch waiting to be closed.

Alexis Rhone Fancher

TLALTECUTLI BY STARLIGHT IN PUERTO ESCONDIDO

I buy her tequila shooters at the Cafe del Mar. She is exquisite, this woman, named for the Mexican goddess of the earth, her eyes the infinity of a moonless night. We're alone at the bar. *I am the unwilling sacrifice,* she cautions. I watch as she swallows the sun. I should heed her warning. Instead, I follow her under the pier, where the wind moans exactly like Tlaltecutli, my lips at her throat, as I tongue my way down her small, brown reticence. *Te quiero,* she sighs, breath the clove of her cigarettes. That night, under the pier, my hunger fueled by tequila and the musk of her hair, I finger her inside her cut-off jeans, embroidered with crossed bones and skulls, while she clings to me, eyes shut, and we sway to the narco-corrido music blasting from some homeboy's boombox, carried on the breeze. It is a steamy September night, the sand still warm from the hot sun's kiss, the beach deserted. Tlaltecutli opens her eyes, two blue-black, smoldering coals. *I am the great Tlaltecutli!* Her deep-throated wail. *Ravish me, plunder me! Tear me apart!* She's crazy drunk, wanton. A vortex, she sucks me in. My mouth finds hers while my fingers bore their way inside her. And when her legs buckle, and her eyes glaze over, I hold her; my fingers impale her until she erupts. Horrified, I watch her body cleave in two. Her arms wrench apart; her agonizing screams pierce the night. I should run, leave her there. But I can't. My legs are sinking in the sand. Tlaltecutli speaks to me with murder in her mouth. *They say nothing will grow until I am moistened with the blood of sacrifice.*

She pulls me down, into her madness. It's where I want to go.

Brian Fanelli

IMAGINING ONE MORE ROMERO MOVIE

I'd like to see Romero's take on *this* moment,
a time as uncanny as the dead rising,
groaning, and slow-walking towards a meal.
The elite already live in towers,
like in *Land of the Dead*.
The president has a tower in NYC,
barricaded by police in all-black riot gear,
like the beginning of a movie
where everything is about to go wrong.
The working-class hustle below,
their hands hard and calloused, their clothes
rife with the smell of gasoline, oil, or dirt.
Sometimes, they crane their necks, stare
at those towers, maybe to imagine a gold nameplate,
a desk, leather chair, and air-conditioned office.

If Romero directed one more sequel,
I wonder where he'd place the survivors.
Shopping malls are too 1980s, but maybe Starbucks,
staring at their smartphones, plugging in
before the dead bust down the doors,
rip out espresso machines, gnaw on flesh,
or maybe he'd have a horde overtake DC,
while afew remaining politicians and lobbyists
flee down K Street under a harvest moon,
until the working-class, turned, drop the gas pumps,
hammers, or call center headsets and devour the living, fed up
with slumping and staggering from job to job.

RELIVING THOSE HORROR MOVIE NIGHTS

I don't want to deconstruct the monster,
or cite Marx to analyze Leatherface's profession,
or Freud to discuss JackTorrance's madness.
I don't want to compare zombies to workers,
rising up to devour the bourgeois in Romero's films,
or count how many masculine traits final girls
must adapt to conquer the slasher.
Save the debate for grad school classes.
I just want to watch the undead
chomp on flesh, or laugh each time
a victim trips in the woods,
fleeing the hockey masked boogeyman.
I want to sit on the edge of the couch,
likeI did when I was a boy,
watching spook films with my father.
I want to find the monster cool again
without explanation, without an essay
linking him to a social class.
Give me the killer's point of view,
knife penetrating flesh, death by proxy, the knowing
I can always shut it off and that behind each impaled body
there is an end credit, an actor and actress who gets to cheat
real death by remaining young on film.
No slasher victim faces what my father faced,
the slowed speech after a stroke, blurred vision,
skin yellowed by cancer. With each re-watch
of *The Thing* or *Night of the Living Dead*, I call forth
his ghost and still see him seated on the couch
next to me, each of us munching popcorn,
awaiting the next kill. In memory, he too
remains younger, one arm stretched out
on the back of the couch, not yet
hooked up to tubes like Frankenstein's Monster
pre-creation. In memory, I can keep him seated
next to me on those Friday nights, before the next scene,
before cancer stalked him, before I learned
not all monsters can be defeated or banished.

SIDING WITH THE BRIDE

I always cheered for the Bride
when she turned to the Creature,
shrieked and refused to wed him,
despite the mad scientist's wishes to breed life.

She didn't need a man to run his fingers
through her tower of hair, those white streaks,
crooked like lightning bolts that brought her to life,
delivered her to the scalpels of a man's hands.

If the Creature didn't pull the lever,
blow up that phallic tower,
declare that he and the Bride
belonged dead because he couldn't have her,

I always imagined that she would have shred
that wedding dress, marched out of that castle,
leaving the men in its shadows, listening to thunder
crack outside and cold rain pelt stone walls.

HanaLena Fennel

HYMNODY IN THE COMMON
after Teeth

Praise the skeletal keepers of
this low belly's howling.
I am primal thing to your love.
Let this be our wedding,
under the muck of the river;
lust instead of breathing.
When they gasp-mouth take what they want
what's the use in waiting?

You are stranger in my wild
cunt low, filled with a lack
of passive fucks to cradle here.
Hitchhike the long way back.
This stable of bodies in my
heather, heath and lilac.
The Sun. You will worship the sun;
until she bites you back.

MICHAEL POWELL'S PEEPING TOM

The camera doesn't rape or even possess, though it may presume, intrude, trespass, distort, exploit and, at the farthest reaches of metaphor, assassinate - all activities that, unlike the sexual push and shove, can be conducted from a distance, and with some detachment.

   —Susan Sontag, *On Photography*

My eyes are not shattering glass windows
or mirrors splintered into red lights,
meaning both stop and for sale at once.
They are screwed up fist punching themselves black.
We say survivor like a carnival booth consolation prize.
It was never soft and hunger-filling as advertised.
I am a vivid slash across the fading of history,
refusing to stay pinned in the photograph,
still screaming *fuck* over and over.

The thing they don't tell you is
some nights are black holes
bookended by an all-teeth shark smile and the turquoise trim of a hotel
you have never seen before;
the only evidence of that night is a picture of you,
still in the bar,
smiling.

The thing about grief nobody tells you is
you resent every step.

There is no way to see the exit from here.

Michael C. Ford

SOMETIMES WE PROVIDE FOR OURSELVES OUR OWN HORROR
after Veda Ann Borg, her movies

The rain goes gray, as only it can in a black and
white fright flick. The old broke bridge collapsed:
just like Carole Lombard's bed in the ironically titled
Nothing Sacred. The eerie screech of *B.F. Goodrich*

and a 4-door sedan is racked-up on a mud flat. Then
three absent-minded scientists, along with one sleek,
spun-gold-haired, hi-fashioned, female tourist
together stand, now, in the murky storm: all the

while, we're seeing brilliant lightning crack the
night revealing this gloomy stone castle with plenty
of guest rooms. Vampires who complain about
working for union scale kiss into the necks of a few

selected Harry Cohn Columbia Pictures contract
players. Yet, nobody remembers you, Veda, except,
maybe, scabs like us who spend our lives waiting for
non-union labor and a pickup truck ride rattling off

to a day gig; those of us
who, still, stand
in our own storms,
every day, in Blood City, California.

Jerry Garcia

AFTER THE INVASION

She wears my wife's apron
but her meatloaf
is without flavor,
and though the 1956 screen-police
will not let us make love,
I assure you
she no longer possesses passion.

In a village demolished by fear,
citizens look vacuous
with an undercurrent of mean.
Parties are sedate affairs
of finger sandwiches and fruit punch.
Even the Catholic parish has relinquished
golden vestments for Geneva drab.

Barbers play crossword puzzles
because hair no longer grows,
faces never shadow.
Beauticians drink tea
since makeup never smudges.
Maids read old comic books,
as glass never spots from rain.

Policemen in pursuit do not use sirens.
There are no heroic measures for gunshots;
the wounded just bleed to death.

AFTER WATCHING DAVID LYNCH MOVIES

Garishly dressed bachelors
leer at women shaped like Dali clocks.
Turnstiles whine like whimpering puppies
as 2 A.M. supermarket shoppers,
those strange hair-netted anomalies,
squint through painfully dilated pupils.
Every sense challenged.

Black clothing offends.
Double "D" sized women, wearing only pasties,
walk suburban streets in daylight.
Accordion grinders materialize on public corners;
grinning monkeys torment
tottering children and housewives.

Everything is a swarthy, luridly red, cocktail lounge.
Illumination is gauzy, vaporous, cigar smoke brown.
Everyone mutters,

even while looking in your eyes.

Michael Gravagno

IT CAME FROM INSIDE THE BRAIN

They're here already.
You're next.

  —Invasion of the Body Snatchers

A rage inside devours without burning.
Hollows out with nothing-teeth
sharpened on everything. Makes innards
inky obsidian. I imagine eyes, black
like a shark. Like cheap sci-fi,
when aliens take control from the inside
and pupils expand into the whole eye.
Black.

In the good movies, the characters fall,
cry in pain, tremor and tremble,
blood spurting from the ear, the mouth.
Points of entry. Before nothing-eyes set in.
If filming takes too long or runs over budget
the characters will just pause
holding breath,
mouth slightly hung in surprise
or ecstasy, the rage swallowing them.
Sometimes, you really do run out
of bubblegum. I'm not afraid
of the anger burning hot.

Listen for the liquid lapping against cement,
for a gurgle or muffled struggle down the hall
before everything seems normal again.
Doubting you heard or saw anything at all
is always a good sign you should stare
up at the vacant, hungry stars
and wait.

Sonia Greenfield

AFTERNOON WITH REDÓN

Odilon, why can't a nymph
learn to love a Cyclops? After all,
we can only focus our two eyes
on the single eye of a lover at any given time.
She would not have to be so shifty;
one to another, the gaze could go unbroken.
His bright blue marble, big as a wheel,
misting over—he'd cry her a lagoon
to bathe in. Why must she just lie there
in molten repose, your damp, vermillion hill
sliding off the canvas? He's got his hungry eye
on her, and he's tragicomic with his clumsy size,
oafish with not knowing right from wrong.
So, Galatea may be a mean girl who thrills
with each rejection, but Polyphemus
is like the rest of us with our imperfect
circumspection. Or he's at the very least
like a monster-hearted boy before he buys
his gun, and she's like the heartbreaker,
the boy-teaser, the self-pleaser
who only thought to have some fun.

FOR SALE: BABY SHOES, NEVER WORN

You think you know the story
but you don't. My baby was born
tentacled. Four legs and two
arms taper to tips, a hybrid form
you might call *freak*, his cupid bow
lips harden like a beak just before
he cries. Golden hued, black slits
darken his eyes. I met his father
in a cave, but before the ink
could clear, all his arms were
pulling me near. Yet I wanted him
ever since I dropped into the deep,
my breath drawn from a tank,
him like shadows through water,
like dreams flowing through sleep.
So no shoes for this boy who reaches
up from my breast, his missing
hands blessed by every tiny cup
that puckers up and suctions a kiss
from my lips. His two tendrils curl
around my smitten face, but it's just
like any other child's embrace.

MILK CARTON KIDS

Now you know they were abducted
on the way to school, past chain-link
urban puzzles, robins scrabbling in the median,
book bags hanging with the weight of history,
or off the side of a rural road in late spring
where slapped mosquitos left smears of horse blood
and the churn of a distant John Deere sounded
like the log-sawing of sleep. Or the teens taken
under the lantern of the supermoon,
by the unused railroad tracks, where flowering
quince unfolds pale pink among
the blackberry brambles and wharf rats
run the length of cool steel in search
of dropped chips. Or in the desert when dusk
slips on her silk nightie, and the saucers
scream like gulls while the aliens shape their ecto
like cacti, go green and prickly. The extra-
terrestrials tap their feet to snap on
high-beams, but we call them stars. Up the kids go
as your radio loses its tune, the television
becomes a box of static, and the digital clock
blinks five again and again. Not stuffed
in a trunk, not dragged from a lake.

WOMEN AND CHILDREN FIRST

When the wind changes direction,
smoke shifts from the fires, so sometimes
it's burning tires in my face, other times
it's meat. Reader, I have done what I can
for you. Gave you my extra Sig
& taught you how to shoot, showed you
which mushrooms are safe to eat, even
trained you to avoid congregations
of carrion flies & the decay they make
love to. If food was plentiful, I shared it.
If the moon only shone on empty woods
or handfuls of bright sequins drummed up
by breeze across the lake, we laughed at
nothing in particular. Now, there's a menace,
a madman pulling off each fence board
at the rear of the yard & I'm crouching
with you, a few bullets left between us.
Reader, I have this child clinging to my leg,
his eyes crazed with fear, his sweaty face
flecked with dirt. The sounds of splintering
wood & hound-like baying make our hackles
rise. You look to me for help, but my field
of vision narrows, only able to take in
the one I would kill to save. I love you,
but you know how it has to be. Grab your
gun, Reader. Run, Reader. Lakshmi Singh
says the hordes are on the move &
from this point on you're dead to me.

Seth Halbeisen

8 THINGS YOU NEVER KNEW ABOUT MEDUSA'S UNDERWEAR

1.
It wasn't always just for show,
a tattered string circling snakelike hips.

2.
There was a time
when men would kill,
just to catch a glimpse.

3.
They were received
as a gift of passion,
a grace upon the world.

4.
They were crafted of
the sheerest golden silk,
which clung like a second skin.

5.
They once provided
glorious stiffness,
unending stamina,
and a masterful
sexual experience.

6.
With them, she gathered
many dedicated followers,
each wrapped in glorious rapture.

7.
They were once the gateway
to the most glorious of treasures,
only to be transformed by jealousy
into a twisted mockery
of what had once been.

8.
Now they are but an ugly reminder,
of a time before the snakes.
Before the loneliness,
the darkness,
and unforgivable sin.

WHY YOU NEVER MAKE DEALS WITH MONSTERS

Because they always know.
Know just what YOU want.
That's what I keep forgetting,
like I always do.
So, now I'm an errand boy.
Shuffling up this mountain,
to a place that doesn't exist.
Not anymore.
A government place.
A thoroughly hellish place.
All for holding tank #4,
more accurately what's inside it.
God, I hope it's small.
That it doesn't wriggle,
or bite,
or is alive.
I have already accepted that it'll be slimy.
It's always slimy.
Always covered in ichor,
smelling to high heaven,
like death twisted sideways
and smothered in gravy.
God, I hate gravy.
It has something to do with their tongues.
How it can taste things beyond this dimension.
Some professor explained it,
that it's non-Euclidean,
so I punched him.
Like knowing that would help me.
Help me get out of its contract.
Help me get my life back.
Before I called it up.
Before I reached too far.

LeAnne Hunt

MERMAID: THE ENDING

She turned her scales fishlike
to shred my hand.
I would not let go
of her tail, her hips, that rhythm
pounding in my blood,
the seas beckoning me
to drown in salty want.
This is love—
the choking.
I bathed in her scent,
swallowed her waters
and rode on her riptide.
She had hooked me,
a gaping fish, so I bound her
in nets, in demands,
in words.
This is love, I said,
the thrashing.
But oceans are never still, and
waves take as much as they give.
I never trusted the moon.
Even with blinds drawn,
I felt the tide rise
behind her eyes. I tried to kiss
away the depths.
I sank to her bottom.
This is love—
the making.
With her breasts pressed against me
and one hand pulling me down,
I never saw the other rise
or the silver flash.
Adrift in my red sea,
I feel the fluttering of slits
along my throat.
This is love—
the breaking.

WHEN WE MAKE GODS AND MONSTERS, WE BREAK THE CHISEL AGAINST OUR BONES AND BRING FORTH LIFE AND DEATH

Mary Shelley knew creators and monsters—
knew they shared the same flesh
stitched by hubris, or worse, by hope.
She knew dead children—
an infant daughter dead at eight-days-old
another daughter, barely a year
a son "sweeter and dearer every day" who died at three
a miscarriage that nearly carried her out of this world.
She knew the act of consuming life
and bringing it forth into a sprinkle of ash.
But she made a world
and one son who lived
out of a creator's poetic spark
and a monster's traitorous flesh.

I too know creation and death
and monsters of our own making—
a son who smiled sweetly but never breathed
a daughter who breathes but whose mouth is cat-fanged
a marriage that almost carried me out of this world
until it alone died
The monster in the bed is worse than the one under it,
but the monster in the mirror
is the one that cannot be escaped.
One monster begets another.
The rage that I swallowed
screams from my daughter's throat.
Her father's blue eyes stitched onto my face.
His long limbs attached to my mannerisms
and twisted by my anxiety.
My rage, his arrogance, my dumb animal pain,
his rending logic and all the violence
in thought and deed
built into one body that each of us chases across the years.
I fear and love what we've wrought.
I pray she will outlive her makers
and create a better world than her monsters.

Arminé Iknadossian

VAGINA DENTATA

How strange, I say as I trace his life-line down
to a diamond cuff-linked wrist.
I'm not wearing any panties.
His right hand reaches for a pound of flesh,
viscosity, and an open door.
Deeper I slur until I have him by his manicured fingertips,
then his knuckles, his delicate wrist.
When he screams, I lick my lips and steady my martini.
I rip his red tie off his fat neck.
Inch by inch, I crush and swallow.
Part woman, part anaconda, I have learned
to digest the unsavory in silence.
I plant my heels as his shoulders fold into me,
unhinge my pelvis to make room for his hips,
and then the rest of him, an anti-birth.
When his mouth is muffled at last,
I tear the toupee off his head
and toss it out the window.
I cough up the bones to give to the people.
We will make toothpicks and lily-white combs.
There is nothing left but his belt, his shoes,
a wedding band rolling down the marble hallway.

Victor D. Infante

HORROR MOVIE TOLD IN TAROT READINGS

1. The Star: A young, nude woman draws water from the lake with a cup. This is the mystery from which we all emerge, beauty and the precipice of sex.

2. The Devil: We'd expect that he would be less like ourselves, this Beast. We fear our reflection, betrayed by what we should trust, *love* being something to chain.

3. The Fool: There is supposed to be wisdom in this moment of hanging. If that is true, it's the wisdom of the grave, the moment a monster's recognized.

4. Death: There was never any other outcome, but then, there never is. Some say this is only *change*. That's nervous whistling to ward off nightmares.

5. Judgment: When we awake to the accusing stares of the dead. We survived. We should be done with screaming. Our screams were buried in a shallow grave.

6. The Hierophant: is a lie and always has been. The haunted have no absolution. This offer of salvation just another form of bondage. We seek The Star, but she's vanished.

7. The Lovers: past position. We remember what we were. We were capable of beauty. We were so alive we near exploded, before everything was consumed by shadows.

8. Unreadable: Call it the Heroin Addict, The Suicide Bomber of the Broken Misogynist Boy. Call it the American President, or the The Studio Executive. Don't give him a name's dignity.

9. The Tower: There is no learning to live inside a burning house. We must leap, and scream and survive when everything is ablaze. There is wisdom in this free fall, if we live to tell the tale.

Jeanette Kelly

THE WHY OF IT

i had forgotten
what it was to be alone
swimming in my black lagoon
gills and scales bathed in liquid life

        above
        feathered creatures
        tree branches hanging low

        beneath
        dark deep rotted limbs
        decaying leaves

i feast and rest among
plants and rocks

until that day
i first saw her reflection
peering over the boat's side
embracing my home she dives
breaking the surface with ripples
body smooth and silvery like the soft
belly of the fish i love to tear
and devour

under her
as she moves across the water
arms rise into the air
fall below the surface
my arms rise
almost touching
stroke for stroke we repeat the same
mirrored patterns again and again
i can feel the trails and spaces
left by her body

        if i let her leave
        i will know alone again

Ron Koertge

DEAR DRACULA

This diet of yours is so cool. Just a pint a day and I'm like
really thin. My old boyfriends are totally after me now, but
no way! All they ever wanted was you-know-what and
make it quick. God, the way you licked my wrist! You
took hours.

I told my mom those holes in my neck were a fad,
like nose rings. She bought it! And don't worry
about Dad. He's so checked out, the walking
dead if you know what I mean.

I can't wait for tonight, Count D. Will you do the
thing with your cape? I love that. And then we
have to chat. My folks are after me to go to city
college. But now I couldn't stay awake in class,
anyway, and if I'm going to live forever, what's
the hurry, right?

I've been thinking, though—I want to be special,
not just another long, white neck. Let's face it. You're
like 9,000 years older than me. You've really been
around. So maybe when we fly back to your castle
in Pennsylvania, I should at least go to night school.

We'll talk, okay? Right now I have to put the crucifix
away, throw a towel over the mirror, then get into
my jammies. Oh, and brush my teeth which, I have
to tell you, seems to take a little longer all the time.

MRS. VICTOR FRANKENSTEIN

She's modeled every nightgown
in her trousseau. Even the sheer
one that made her mother faint.

Instead of kissing her, Victor scolds her:
"A storm is coming. Tonight of all
nights, you must stay in your room!"

Then she's alone with her needlework
and the harpsichord. Again.

The thunder is a relief. She goes onto her
balcony and lets the rain pummel her.
Lightning makes night into day.

She hears heavy footsteps on the stair,
footsteps that pause, at last, outside
her door.

As the door is torn from its hinges,
she undoes a few buttons and pinches
her cheeks harshly to bring on a blush.

THE ABOMINABLE SNOWMAN

Up here on the forehead of the world, it's always
cold. On the other hand, there's very little crime.

My wife and I live in a cave way above the snow
line. It's a simple life with no distractions to

speak of. There's lots of foraging. Otherwise
we practice nonchalance. For fun, we leave

footprints and sometimes intriguing scat
a cameraman has to take a close-up of.

There's always a cameraman, part of a team:
one in a Nessie baseball hat and this time

ardent Nora who wants to be the first woman
to photograph us. She thinks the men have

gone about it all wrong and her notes, pinned
to a glacier, are charming: *Help me believe!*

And *I have fire. Really.* In her journal, which I
pilfer while they sleep or hike, Nora's worried

about her hair. She's planned an assignation
with a man she met on the plane. Well, well.

Someone handsomer than I, no doubt. Still,
I like her, so I grunt into a tape recorder

before I leave and urinate in a hat, not the one
she planned to wear for her rendezvous in Bhutan,

I hope.

WEREWOLF, 2000

It used to be when one of my ancestors
looked up at the full moon, he soon found
himself snarling and tearing at someone's
brocade, only to wake the next morning
in another ruined suit.

But over the decades the curse thins,
the blood cools. Now the countess loves
moonlight. She wears loose trousers
and I fetch a stick. We roughhouse
in front of the fire. When she bathes,
I open the door with my smart muzzle
and listen to her sing.

Lying at her feet as she eats from a simple
bowl, I dread the next morning: problems
with the game keeper, servants who steal,
a ball we have to attend, the horrible soup
that begins an endless banquet with us
at either end of a Regency table dressed
to kill and longing for a full moon.

Elmast Kozloyan

WEAVING WEBS

Spindle silk strands
An imbued gift
woven to perfection
Invisible
to a certain slant of light
Erotic tales
laced in spiral threading
Wait

He won't notice at first
until he's tangled in your hard work
Knit knots
Nibble for taste
and seasoning
Bat your eight eyes
wink four
Say that you love him
Devour him whole

Repeat

Pat M. Kuras

AT THE GATES OF HELL

there is a dog
with three heads
named FiFi.
She is a poodle, after all.
Her eyes are liquid,
sometimes teary from
the soot and sulphur and,
on occasion,
she yaps her displeasure
in triplicate.
The fire and brimstone
sully her coat.

Charon is no fun.
He just toodles his boat
back and forth,
depositing newcomers.
FiFi greets them,
her eyes shining,
all three faces
turned up, smiling,
her pompom tail
thumping cheerfully.

The newcomers are
worse than Charon.
They make no note
of her, slink past,
heads bowed,
mournful and depressed.

FiFi has had enough.
Someday she's going to
blow this clamshack,
leap into Charon's boat
and return to the
land of the living.

Hope is a three-headed poodle
at the gates of hell.

Zachary Locklin

I LOVE DEAD. HATE LIVING

I know who made me, and how.
I have learned how to speak, and
how to drink and smoke. I am
capable of enjoying myself. I am
capable of empathy. I do not know
why. I know where I came from
but not who I was, or who I am,
or who I could be. I know I am
alone, which is not the same as
loneliness. Knowing you are alone
is the same as loneliness. I know
that well enough by now.

ITALIAN FILMS...*AM I RIGHT?*

A student makes a joke about the two *Death Walks* movies:
"Is there a crossover where *Death Walks
in High Heels at Midnight?*"

But you have to understand,
the titles to these gialli are:
1) amazing,
and 2) almost always
completely unrelated to
the actual content of the movie.

Short Night of Glass Dolls?
What the fuck
does that even mean?

Although to be fair,
there is a bird with crystal plumage
in *The Bird with Crystal Plumage*,
and there are seven deaths
and a cat
in *Seven Deaths in a Cat's Eye*
(which is admittedly less giallo
and more Italian Gothic).

Your Vice Is a Locked Door and Only I Have the Key
is a strange-ass title for an adaptation
of Edgar Allan Poe's *The Black Cat*,
but there are forbidden photos
of a lady who is above suspicion
in *Forbidden Photos of a Lady above Suspicion*
and somebody does
do something to Solange
in *What Have You Done to Solange?*

Evelyn may or may not
come out of the grave
in *The Night Evelyn Came Out of the Grave*
(no spoilers), and I suppose

somebody does kill seven times
in *The Red Queen Kills Seven Times*,
while the lady in black's
perfume is noteworthy
in *The Perfume of the Lady in Black*.
There is no literal lizard
in a woman's skin
in *A Lizard in a Woman's Skin*,
but, like, metaphorically it works.

Seven Blood Stained Orchids
has seven orchids in it,
however briefly, though
I would say they're more
drizzled in blood
than blood *stained*.

So, I suppose
I have to rethink
my initial hypothesis.

THE TWIN FATES OF HENRY FRANKENSTEIN

The Doctor has been spared!
By order of the studio,
he has been removed from the scene
to stand cowering with Elizabeth
as the Tower collapses.

And yet if you look,
there, against the inside wall,
the white form of his
lab-coated frame
presses back from the flames
and falling rubble.

Who do we believe:
our eyes, or *our* eyes?
The studio, or the script?
Or can both truths somehow
coexist in parallel?
Can we live and die
in equal measure
at all times?

The Doctor has been spared!
But still he presses to the wall
as the ceiling collapses.

Rick Lupert

DRACULA, THIS IS FOR YOU

I've written so many poems for the dead lately.
Robin Williams, dead, he got a poem.
Leonard Nimoy, dead, he got a poem.
Pete Seeger, gone, he got a poem.

I even wrote a poem for Leonard Cohen
who, technically, was not dead at the time,
but, he was getting up there.

But how do you write a poem for the dead
who still walk the earth,
whose story keeps going on?

I'll tell you this, Vlad…May I call you Vlad?
I've seen all of your movies, I feel like we're best friends,
I'm going to go ahead and call you Vlad.

I'll tell you this, Vlad,
My favorite Vampire literature is that told
from the point of view of the vampire.
I'm looking at *you*, Ann Rice.

(I really am looking at her,
she's hovering over my desk while I write this.
Stop distracting me, Ann Rice!)

If I hadn't been assigned to read
"The Vampire Lestat" at, of all places,
a Jewish Undergraduate College,

(I'd always suspected Judaism and vampirism
were much more connected than the literature
of either would have you believe.)

If I hadn't read that book I probably
would have regarded you with the same
general affection as, say, Frankenstein.

But the story of that vampire let me get inside your head.
Even though your story, Vlad is typically told from the point of view
of those who regard you as evil.

I know what's really up. You're a love story.
An immortal being who just wants to hook up
with a little human hottie forever.
I get it.

QUIET, ANN RICE!

So you drink a little blood, or
that's all you ever drink…who doesn't?!
I can't tell you how many times I thirstily open the fridge

and there's my choice…either the Acai juice
from Whole Foods (Knudsen)
or the human blood (which I keep in the fridge for some reason
even though we all know it's better warm…)
It's a tough choice…I get it.

Vlad…The Impaler…and don't worry, I think
the statute of limitations on all the impalings you did
as a human has run out. I mean look "Impalings"
isn't even a word anymore according to *spellcheck*.

You're good. I'm on your side.
So, if you could just bring me on over. I'm ready.
And you don't have to worry, my blood is Kosher.

But take me…I want to see the future.
I put a penny in the bank and I want to laugh
in a thousand years when

I'm the richest guy in Van Nuys.
I want to see what buildings fall
and what empires rise.

I can handle it.
I hardly ever go out during the daylight anyway.
I'm a poet after all, and a freelancer, I work from home.

Take me to the other side Vlad,
we'll find her together.
And I am so thirsty.

Tony Magistrale

WHEN IS IT TIME TO PANIC?

About an hour before I was supposed to go out
and lecture on *The Shining*, the snow
began to pile up, and while I tried
not to act too concerned about this, although it was July,
the street outside my hotel window
had disappeared, not merely swallowed under the heavy snows,
but gone completely, replaced by
a landscape of tall pines, imposing mountains,
the faraway voice of a loon. *What happened to Cleveland?*
I turned to ask my wife,
who was now wearing a cute little black
flapper cocktail dress and veiled hat over brunette wig
and maybe a little too much black lipstick.
Did I do something bad to that annoying little kid
who keeps riding his Big Wheel by the door of our room
at all hours of the night (I've only seen him from behind)
attended by this eerie, sparkly music that sounds
like stars rattling in a xylophone,
because suddenly my wife won't talk to me,
skulking around with a baseball bat
and this raccoon-eyed wild look.
This was about the time
I thought it best to telephone Stanley
and get his clear-eyed directorial input,
when I remembered he was already long gone,
and Stephen King
refused to take any of my calls.

Jennifer Martelli

BLACK PHILLIP INTERROGATES THE SOON-TO-BE-GIGANTIC WOMAN, ONCE CALLED THOMASIN
for Lucie Brock-Broido

Define the word cloven.
Define cleft. How many milk teeth
rooted in your baby brother's jaw?
What to do with the bones
you can't grind down? The thigh. The clavicle. The moon
reflects off the greasy riding stick: the broom.
Coat the whole branch cleft
from the apple tree with Mercy's fatty butter—
isn't it delicious between your lips?
Your cunt is cleft. Is it velvety deep red & gold?
Cleave to the warm knotty branch
with your tight thigh muscles. Do you
still cleave to God? Your father's cleft
mind, his cleft chin. Did he lie? Did he lust?
How many cords of wood did he cleave with his ax?
Is he beset with the silver cup of pride?
Did your mother drink from it? Is her milk
bloody? She can't tell a crow from a child. In her womb
twins cleaved, were cloven, were born & cleft.
Her golden hair cleaved down the middle, cloven-tongued
snakes, she lactated black milk & blood. Cleave.
Can you see the tops of the trees? The low
yew, the apple trees, the maples, the white pines
with soft nuts deep within the bone-hard
brown cones? See the branches lit
by the moon big as Salem. Do they scratch
your belly & gore? My horns curl introspective & fatal,
they point back. Do you see my irises? Split &
gold & cleft, they let in dark dilation. A small loom—
a tatting shuttle will fit in the palm of your hand.
See how it fits snug as your labia majora like a
constellation twisting in the sky orgasmic over the Puritan
night. Can you tat lace for your pretty red dress? Define cleave.
Do you like mulled cider? Define clove. Can you

smell it? Here, see? In the clearing—
your legs spread like the cloven limbs of the high
trees. Can you stand it? Do you know
what it is to be cleaved & gigantic?

Rise rise rise rise up & up & up & up
cleft from the breathing ground of this place.

HERMAN MUNSTER KNOWS HE'S HANDSOME

All of the world's happiness hangs from the spider webs
on his neck bolts. Wherever he stands, the sun

rises and sets at the horizon line of his head. All of the world's
knowledge ends at the point of his wolf-boy son's widow's peak.

His wife loves him, and so he is beautiful. Lily understands
how the world beyond 1313 Mockingbird Lane is confused, and so

her hair is black streaked white: you either love or you don't. She is kind
to the blondes, the blue-eyed nieces, the dimwitted. You and I may call it

condescension, but it is love. Her father sucks our blood
and ichor runs warm and blue through his veins: he turns us all into gods

after we're dead. She lets the dragon out at night from under the stairs
and it lights the way: bonfires ignite the black pines. The whole town

gathers at the end of the darkest days. Mockingbirds
hop weightless on her shorn lawn, behind the iron gate.

THE SACRIFICE

Not the bees!

    —Nicolas Cage, *The Wicker Man*

Nobody knows it's me. I am wearing a full-grown doe's head.
I pulled cut crystals off the chandelier, hung them from my white birch antlers.
I am wearing her pelt (not real, golden felt squares patched & stitched
myself). Nobody is unsafe. My eyes are slit like my cats',
like the eyes of the small black goat, slit brown velvet.

I wanted to wear my Anjou pear costume, the velour purple red one,
hide in the branches of the tree outside the house where people plot, then dance.
I wanted to bruise easily like fruit left fallen under the trees in autumn.
There wasn't a color close enough—not really blue, not the color of a dull
knife tarnished, not the tarnish, not the color of the lead core of a nub.

Not the color of skin under the eyes of a menstruating woman.
I wanted to dress as a narrative—an arc the shape of a breast, the good one
that grows over a heart in a rib cage. They found the old mask, bent
wire and latched fontanel to pour the bees down, coating a whole
moon face: a black veil that molds.

The townsfolk gather to watch in a field of sweet grass. Now I am milkweed silk.
My skin, soft as burnt butter, warm, easy to rip open. All along, Plath
knew betrayal by one was betrayal by all, by the whole town red
blushing stomach sac, deep & strewn as a pomegranate. Here is the body. Here
is the mid-fall altar. Plath cried at the end she was cold, but no, here

it is warm I swear it is swollen & shamefully warm.

Carrie McKay

DO NOT PANIC

Stay in your homes.
Do not let them see you.
Turn off the lights.
Close curtains and blinds.

Do not use water.
Do not use power.
Do not leave your home.
Do not panic.

The message repeated
over and over
until the batteries gave out,
solar panels darkened.
Until silence.

Time and again
we radioed sound, pictures,
and molecular patterns
to the foreign stars.

When the Hydrogians left,
carrying the carbon extractions
mined from the last humans,
they flew past the waves of
Earth's first message to Space.

Too slow.
Too soon.
Too late.

LATE NIGHT PHONE CALL FROM CHESSIE

Hello, my brother.
Have you forgotten me?
Do the many years stand between us
like the miles between air and sea floor?

I'd like to forget you too;
to disbelieve in oil wells spewing poison
that holds the air from my heart.
I'd like to forget boats and nets
that harm my true friends.

You never did understand;
Why I left you without a word.
Why I took the children
deep and far from your reach.

You are so far from nature,
even your scales have abandoned you.
So out of balance that
you flood the land with your greedy seed
making room only for yourself.

I tried to forget you and
the poison promises of those before you.
It's hard to forgive when
your children cough black late into the night.

You've forgotten the power of a tail,
the strength of my coiled hug
and the force of my waves.

Take cover, climb high,
build and build again.
With each thrash of my tail
the ground will shake
and the bay rise to fill your homes.

Taste the oil that flavors our every breath.
The Sea is taking back its home.

WE WILL LEAVE THESE JARS

I love your meninges.
I love the way I imagine it would feel
to my sensory receptors -
so soft and slippery.
The neuron stimulus is beyond…
beyond years of knowledge to explain,
even if I had words.

My basal ganglia reach out
to the ears you no longer have.
My neural transmitters call you closer,
to awaken the love and even lust
in your parietal lobes.
I love all your lobes.

And some day, more
than just our shared fluids
and hormones will touch.
Someday, our cerebellums will awaken
to our new, healthy bodies.
We will leave these jars
and once again touch.

Lincoln McElwee

FALLING FOR THE END OF THE WORLD AGAIN

I'm traveling to you. I'm scared. I'm falling for the end of the world again. And I can't get to you fast enough, I'm afraid that if the big bad moon really blows into orbit or we awaken angry Martians while mining for life on Mars, that if vampires get smart and blow up the sun (or if they really do sparkle!), or if any of these TV zombies finally unleash their damned zombie apocalypse, I need to be in bed with you, where things still won't make sense but where at least I've worked for the ending. The corner market is a suburban wet dream where liquor, Xanax and STD kits shimmer in an oasis of instant ramen, flavored rubbers and white rice. Greeting cards line the rows like tombstones tagged by ad execs. I move through the store picking up two-ply and vodka because I need to feel comfortably numb, and when I'm stressed or nervous I shit and drink in no particular order. The end of the world is a deathbed where we're handcuffed to the bedposts like lovers. There's no safety word for this, because pain is a sixth sense sniffing at our soiled mortality. I make it to the park near the church in Placentia, the place where I confessed to you about my rocky relationship with the sky. And I really am tired of the sky always falling like a nursery rhyme on repeat. My arms can't reach up to be of any use. I'm just too short to give a shit. You told me how you'd like to feel bad for both the chicken and the egg but this damn eggshell of a world's always ending again. We're always panning with these existential crises. But I'm almost there, where you are, at the end of the world. When I get there, you'll tell me there's no longer need for papers or passports. You'll tell me to forget about Mars and zombies and oddly-sparkling pretty things, that tone-deaf sky always falling. You'll tell me that the end of the world will always end because time is such a gluttonous cannibal. And I'll listen. I'll eat it up. I'll purr like a fat cat in a new wonderland. Our world will end, big banged, together. I'll close my eyes in bed while you stamp me instead with a kiss. It won't be admission, just pressed confession. It'll say, *you were here when it happened*. It'll be signed, *deep down I wanted this*.

Daniel McGinn

EVERYBODY KNOWS A WOLF CAN'T SMILE

A wolf walks at her side, growing with the shadows, stretching his big bad self across the woods, loping smoothly with a six-tree stride. The fur on his back is wild and electric, not soft and pretty like the hair that slips in haphazard curls from between Red's hood and cape. The wolf has forgotten about the basket of goodies and is fixated on the scent of little girl blood. His paws move silently. His ears stand erect. He focuses on footsteps, twigs snapping and the commingling of breath that joins the girl to the animal. Look at the moon resting on Red's riding hood as if she were the source of light and look at the wolf, housed in darkness, hidden by trees, his eyes lit bright and yellow like a blackbird that waits and watches and smiles.

SHE PAINTED HER NAILS

She painted her nails black.
She wanted them to match her lips.

She painted her nails with a hammer,
pain was the house she was building.

She painted her nails and hands
and her arms slid out of the canvas,

she grabbed the watcher by the rib cage
and made him crack and splinter.

She painted her nails in blood;
blood drawn from the river.

She painted her nails with a broomstick
and she cackled as she did it.

Ally McGregor

ALIENS LIKE CHOCOLATE MILK

Sometimes I wonder why
aliens abduct cows;
what they could possibly offer
an extraterrestrial lifeform
as they roam fields with chunks
of grass between their teeth,
mooing at shadows shaped
like butcher knives,
while shrugging off the paranoia
of being tipped over
by a group of high-school
students, bored after prom.

My friend once said,
as I was obsessively inquiring,
Everyone loves milk.

I imagined a lone cow,
with large, watery eyes
turned towards the sky,
thinking the glowing, neon light
beaming down from a spaceship
is the sparkling hand of God,
reaching to levitate her away
from her life on the dairy farm—
because she's covered in feces,
her legs buckle when she walks,
and she hasn't seen her baby
in months.

What took you so long?

Only then for her to be violated
by long, cold fingers
greedily probing
at swollen udders,
before being dropped back to Earth,
a crop-circle left as a receipt,
because she wasn't chocolate-flavored.

Ryan McMasters

TRUTH OR DARE MOVIE RESPONSE

Truth: I used to be lonely.

Truth: I love watching movies by myself.

Dare: I need the filmmakers of the *Truth or Dare* movie to inform me why a guy kissing a guy is as dangerous as a woman getting shot in the head since they both can't be seen on screen, but a woman kissing a woman is totally acceptable?

Truth: I like kissing more than I thought I would.

Truth: Straight women caricaturing the lesbian experience gets more positive attention than the lesbian experience.

Dare: I dare everybody to ask themselves why coming out to a homophobic parent was a plot in a scary movie that, again, couldn't have airtime?

Truth: I told one sister I liked guys this December.

Truth: I told the other one a few days ago.

Dare: Tell me why the shooting of a gay man is viewed in the movie, but nothing else is seen except his hiding?

Truth: I am morphing into an angry gay; my identity recoils when everyone wants to take a shot.

Truth: I want people to be stronger & braver than I am regarding the truth they possess.

Dare: I dare you to survive into a generation where homophobes fear us for legitimate reasons as opposed to made up ones,

and it's all on screen.

José Enrique Medina

MUTATION

This is not the dream in which, engulfed in the cotton
of fog, beside the husky sea, you hear the tap-tap-tap

of a red-tipped cane, inventing a path
for the blind old Japanese man, and you sit

at his side, listening to his fishing adventures
when he had youth and sight.

No. This time's different. In this dream,
you are a purple octopus, stranded on the beach,

by the crystal of a wave. Medusa's head,
washed ashore. Your arms undulate,

wrinkling the water which, except
for the little rays of riding stars, is invisible.

Each headlong breaker rearranges your tentacles
into a new expression of grief. Your side

gills snort and flap, choking on furry air.
White fog drifts. A white smudge moves—

a man wearing white? You're almost blind.
In this dream, without ears, plucked out of the hug of liquid,

trembling in the dryness, you don't hear any sound.
That's why, when the young Japanese man

approaches you with his hooked spear, silently,
your three hearts palpitate, as if he were the last wave.

NIÑOS DE LA TIERRA

I grew up believing there were children under the earth.

"When it rains, they come out," Abuelita said, wrapped in the exoskeleton of her black rebozo. "One sting, and you're dead."

After a storm, my little brothers and I guarded the windows with plastic swords, watching mud shining in moonlight.

"They're bald like a new-born," Abuelita whispered with her mothball breath. "They cry like a child."

We listened, between wind's pauses, for their wail.

If we broke a plate, she frowned, her face wrinkled like caterpillar-skin.

"They have six legs and little baby fingers at the end of each leg. They kidnap bad kids."

We hid, blankets curled around us like cocoons.

Covered in church-veil cobwebs, she slammed her hand against the door. We huddled together. "Don't go outside. The children of the earth are going to get you."

"What are they?" we asked.

"They're Satan's children. Part baby, part tiger."

One day, I flipped her the middle finger.

"I'm going to grab that little finger and twist it and give it to the earth babies." She grimaced. "They'll drag you to hell."

When Abuelita died, we put dead cockroaches in one of her shoe boxes, and buried it in the garden. We sealed her grave with water we said was holy, trapping her underground.

All that summer we ran on top of her, laughing, surrounded by swollen roses.

R.S. Mengert

ELEGY FOR GODZILLA

"Gorilla Whale" they called you in vernacular, an affront
to logic they could not control, and thus a monster.

With your luminescent scales, your breath of fallout fire,
you were the picture of the Nemesis – that western dragon

of revenge against a blazing life of chaos never asked for.
Atomic science made you, blasted you awake

and gave a dazzling glow to your reptilian hunger,
set in motion the machinery of a cold, three-chambered heart.

"Godzilla has a brain this big," said the scientist
holding up a pea. He sounded smug, American, words

that did not match the movement of his lips
while ordering your execution in the watery grave

from which you lumbered forth as his brilliant mistake.
His taciturn gray suit and horn-rimmed specs

belied an arrogance, an unearned certainty of purpose.
And while it's true you were not smart, nor beautiful,

nor capable of warmth, you had a dignity
that only comes with rage, a purity of thought and motive

rendering you graceful as you swept your shark-finned tail
across a toy tank army, trampled down a cardboard Tokyo,

while he cringed, safe and clean in a sound-stage bunker,
deliberating as he washed his slender hands.

ELEGY FOR KONG

Free from human company, you had a perfect darkness
in the forest, nothing to fear

but ordinary death. From that, they took you to the idiotic awe
of crowds, white lights through iron bars.

What else could you do but grab
the first thing you saw that wasn't loathsome, the woman

who acknowledged your awareness, the human
who could tell you were alive, and scale with her a tower

to the emptiness of clouds, the ants
a mile below you in their cars, looking up in terror.

What else could you do but swat the war-planes
they had sent to sting you back to earth.

Brother Ape, your death, though glorious, will not redeem the race
that laid you low. Nor will you come again to judge.

But in that moment, you lived among us, hanging from a needle's tip
above oblivion, a life clutched dear in one hand,

dealing death out freely with the other.

Ryan Meyer

THE OLDEST RULES IN THE BOOK

The kids couldn't sleep
so they pulled out
an old Ouija board
to have someone new
to talk to.

An old soul responded
to: *is anyone there*
with a simple *yes*.
The doors opened.

It wasn't long before the
kitchen cabinets slammed closed
at night and the chairs scraped loud
across the wooden floors.
They felt tickling sensations on their skin
and whispers in their ears
as they slept.

The invited slithered in through
every crack in the floorboards and
every hole in the walls,
filling them with history
of the oldest rules in the book:

don't make any calls without reason,
and don't expect guests to arrive
without friends.

Bill Mohr

AT THE GLOBAL MULTIPLEX

"Do you really want
to see *The Babadook?*"
"A part of me is curious,"
I say. "Which part?" "The look /

don't look" parting of
the red sea of climate change.
The planet is a pop-up book:
glaciers melt, but I don't cringe.

Flip a page and watch the rain
forests spewing brittle kites
of ashes from the haunted stain
of a hundred thousand acres burnt.

Not everyone gets to relax
at this movie for free. I must confer
some distance with my purchased snacks
for Irony, like Nature, to endure.

THE GHOUL CONVENTION

"The young ones can't catch on. Stay calm,
even when confronted with the hilarious panic

of a half-dead corpse. After waiting all year,
don't leave the picky eater picnic with any regrets."

The old ones give each other shoulder rubs
while reading back issues of *Ghoul Housekeeping*.

Next year's panels are announced: Topiary Management.
("Even a ghoul must plant his garden.")

Wraith of the year! Eidolon of the decade!
The world is not an ugly place, not yet.

No natural enemies, a voiceover recites.
A very young ghoul is digging holes in a huge field

too far from any city to be a place for mourning,
yet the bereft come here to be alone, or grouse.

"Ignominy," an adolescent mutters. "Carnival music,"
a widow responds. "Casual acquaintances,"

their companions proclaim. "Whores for hire
in all but name." "Depends on your definition

of virginity," said a half-naked ghoul getting dressed
again. "I don't like accidents," the seduced insist.

"Unintentional carnage is so boring, so effete."
"Magnanimous spite is the only motive I respect."

Borrowing the sentiments of triumphant candidates,
the ghouls repay their debts with orphaned toys.

Eric Morago

FROM NANCY, TO FREDDY

How many years has it been since I'd burn skin to stay awake—
to keep from sleep and you? The nightmare ended a lifetime ago;

my bed is no longer a fist of knives, and yet at times, I miss their threat
and tingle along my spine—the hero you made of me. But now, without you,

my monster, *what am I*? I drink soy decaf lattes with girlfriends, gossiping
over Instagram posts and Twitter feeds. I have too much red wine with dinner,

enough to promise I fall fast asleep. I don't dream. Remember the boiler room?
How you'd chase me—a ballet of flames reflecting in your eyes. Your blistered

face, a bouquet of scars. Your smile, a snake. How do I get back *there*?
I want to feel fear in my mouth again, swallow its electricity until I glow

courage. Give me your cackle and taunts—your wolf's breath at my door,
all huff and puff. Play me a song of razors scraping metal pipes like

the strumming of synthesized guitar. I need a soundtrack for my comeback,
something that builds and builds and builds. *God*, I am so bored these days,

I swipe right for every man in a striped sweater, hoping their fingers,
on my flesh, are just as sharp as yours. When I ask if, in their bedroom,

they hide a furnace that I can fight my way out of, I am disappointed
when they always say no—relieved when they never call again.

Don't you feel it's about time for a sequel? I think tonight I'll brew
a pot of dark roast and draw myself a hot bath. I'll let down my guard,

enough to make things interesting. I can see it now—the struggle
to stay alert that only pulls one closer to sleep—the drip and sizzle,

your hand creeping out of the water like a secret, the faint hum
of children singing a lullaby: *one, two, Freddy's coming for...*

YOU'RE A GOOD ZOMBIE, CHARLIE BROWN

It started with Woodstock—some mutated strain
of bird flu. His first victim, Pig Pen, tasted terrible,
but the hunger was just too overpowering to care

about good hygiene. Next Peanut down was Marcie—
cleaning her glasses, she never saw it coming. Upon
infection, she went straight for Peppermint Patty.

You always hurt the ones you love, sir. When they
came for Charlie Brown, he thought, *Good grief,*
wondered if MetLife had him covered as both girls

undressed the flesh from his bones. This was not
the threesome he wanted. His sister, Sally, heard
his screams across the hall and cried hysterically.

Cried not for herself, but because she knew who
she would go to when she turned. But Linus,
not wanting to go out like that, did what he must—

took his blue blanket, fashioned a noose around
his neck, and hung himself from the ceiling fan.
Sally scratched for days at a door to a quiet room.

Snoopy showed more courage and jumped atop
his dog house to take aim at Charlie Brown's
half-eaten head. Though by the time he realized

his dogfights with Red Baron were all pretend,
it was too late. Blood splattered everywhere—
Snoopy became invisible beside his red home.

Lucy, seeing there was money to be made
in times of a zombie apocalypse, increased
her cost for psychiatric help to 15 cents, but

soon regretted it when a reanimated Snoopy
came for her brain. She was always terrified
of his kiss—more so now—tried outrunning

him, but it wasn't long before he was lapping
her cheek with his tongue, then chewing it off
with his teeth. Her only consolation was that

in death she finally could have what she wanted
in life—Schroeder, all to herself, away from his
toy piano. She ate his fingers first, like taquitos.

Through it all he continued to play—banged
his bloody stumps against the tiny ivory keys
until every bit of Beethoven left his body.

The sole survivor of the group, Franklin, who
having no anxiety or obsession to distract him,
saw this horror show coming and escaped, long

before his friends noticed he'd gone. He refused
to be killed off that way—consumed like cliché,
becoming just another monster, same as them.

Eileen Murphy

the monster

father!
he wakes up on a slab
with the doctor
hovering over him with a probe
& he knows that he is composed
of scraps of other human beings
sutured together
& that electricity
is somehow involved
as are the flasks in the lab
that catch the half-light that falls
through the barred basement windows
& he has the impulse
to flee out-of-doors
run naked through the tree-lined streets
maybe meet some friendly villagers,
but when he tries to sit up
he finds he is restrained hand & foot
by leather straps
for your own good
intones the doctor
who knows a lot more about
villagers than the monster does

Ashley Naftule

HAIKUS BY JASON VORHEES

1.

If you had a face
like mine, you'd wear a hockey
mask all the time too.

2.

You think your mom is
embarrassing? My mom killed
Kevin Bacon! Yeesh.

3.

My daily workout:
stalk, chase, stab, Gatorade break.
Stalk, chase, stab, hack, slash.

4.

Despite what you've heard,
I've got nothing against teen sex.
I just hate teens.

5.

I started using
Tinder. I always swipe right…
With my machete.

Robbi Nester

MERMAID TO WOMAN

In the ocean's wavering light,
seen from above, her body
wears a human form, its crests
and hollows womanly.
And yet the mimicry remains
imperfect, her shape resembling
the swell and sudden falling off
of breakers in a storm, her striped
teeth those of a parrot fish,
suitable for tearing flesh,
dorsal fin a frill between
sharp shoulder blades,
wild octopus eyes.
All her life she sang ships straight
into the rocks, but could not help
pitying the sailors, far from home,
drawn by voices that promised so much.
A predator in love with her prey,
she envies their shapely calves,
longs to enfold them in her own
strong thighs, to scissor the waves
and step out on shore.
She's only held their drowned
and swollen bodies.
Just once, she wants
to touch their living skin,
to scrape the glittering scales
from her long arms, her hands.
She would give up anything,
her sweet voice, bright carpet of corals
and anemones, duets with whales
to be one of those alien others
striding the green world.

SEA STAR

after a painting by Jennifer Ninnis

We have heard of selkies and mermaids,
women who shed the burden of their human
skin and take the form of sea creatures, seals
or hybrid beasts. But no fabulist I know of
has yet imagined that a woman might embrace
a sea star's form. Invertebrate, radially symmetrical,
moving so oddly on its myriad feet it seems
a composite rather than a single beast, this
creature has an eye on every arm. It has
the power to regenerate its parts, and sometimes,
cut in half, has been known to mend its body
if the vital organs have been spared.
Anyone might envy this power. So perhaps
it's not surprising that the woman in the deck
chair, weary of her life on this side of the ocean,
might desire a sea star's life, so she gradually
assumes this form, lengthening first one leg,
then another. Her hair retreats into her scalp,
the neck and head preparing to become
yet another arm. In one last action of her
human mind, she sends a message in a bottle
into the surf, telling her story to the waiting world.

Martina Reiz Newberry

UNIDENTIFIED FLYING OBJECTS

Ageless in the dark,
a young woman is enthralled

by the paranormal
as if it was next to her in bed.

She longs for a ghost story of her own,
some strange thing to mull over

in her insomniac hours. The radio says,
They're coming for all of us in the dark.

They'll come in their silver cylinders,
their silver suits. Their huge black eyes

will stare through us. Ageless in the dark,
she hollows out a space in her heart

for these great-eyed creatures. They are as far
from sleep as she is, intrigued by dark as she is,

foreign as she is and still they are untroubled. She is not.
The radio ups its own volume. *In just a minute you'll hear*

the sounds of an actual UFO landing
and the cries of those watching it.

She waits through a commercial and another
and still another, waiting for sounds she'll never hear.

Terri Niccum

"LIZZIE BORDEN TOOK AN AX AND GAVE HER MOTHER 40 WHACKS"

"40 whacks" *is* an exaggeration,
and she never was my mother,
but my *father's wife*. I took a few extra divots
to make sure, never 40. She'd
come upstairs—up that flight of steps
that creaked and narrowed—
to criticize how I'd made a bed. Really!
Something I'd been doing all my life.
Something they kept me around to do
even though we had a live-in maid,
that and to dust the occasional gewgaw,
the bit of cheap bric-a-brac my father
would barely allow even his second wife
to buy. Father—who kept me
dressed in past years' and jumble-bin clothes
until buttons popped and holes
made the church crowd blush—
believed children should be
seldom seen and less heard,
forbade parties and only granted me
a day off on Sunday to sit beside him
on a hard pew and scowl at the hymnals.
Father now, he might have merited
41. He'd come in from a walk
after my warmup and missed the screams.
Down he lay on the couch for a nap.
I helped him loosen his shoes,
even brought him a pillow for his head.
He looked so peaceful there,
and once I decided he should never get up,
I hefted, swung, and covered him
with blood. I even cleaved the stern eye
he'd pinned on me for years.

THE 50-FOOT WOMAN RETELLS IT

You couldn't call me big boned.
That just wouldn't cover it.
In fact, when I blossomed into a 50-foot
Big Girl with vitals to match,
I had a hard time covering all
my lady parts. I wasn't being immodest—
curtains and bedsheets
just don't stretch that far.
And I wouldn't have left the house
if they hadn't kept trying to chain me up
and poke me with needles.
But what I want to know
is why everyone thought I was the villain
and not my philandering husband?
Just because five linebackers
could have used one of my breasts for an awning,
was that any reason to wrap
me in iron and wimpily try to sedate me?
And, prior to my growth spurt,
what did I ever do wrong
other than amass 50 mill
that my rat husband Harry
wanted to share with that summer stock floozy,
Honey Parker? Oh, sure, I tippled a bit
and was fond of midnight drives alone in the desert.
I guess that was my downfall—not running
when the saucer planted its light
within yards of my car,
when that enormous hand reached out
and all I could do was scream.
Oh well. Aside from the nuisance
of needing to play kickball with a few trucks
trying to block my way downtown, for a while
it felt good to be the woman in power,
to really hear the roar
of my thunder thighs,
to rip the roof off the bar
where Harry and his bitch were hiding

and make that gaslighting husband of mine
squeak with fear. Oh, and when I lifted that ceiling beam
like a pickup stick and dropped it on Honey—
CRUSH! SMUSH! What a rush!
After that as in all good 50s movies,
the writing was on the wall.
But at least I got in
one last grab for Harry.
And so, when that exploding power tower
torched my 50-feet, I was ready
to lay down my arms,
open my hand and expose that bounder
squashed like the bug he was.
After all, he tried to shoot me!
And though the bullets bounced right off,
it hurt my feelings.
And really big girls have really big feelings.

Andrew November

POLTERGEIST HAIKU

Zelda Rubenstein
can clean my house anytime.
That sexy, squeak voice.

Martin Ott

VOICES OF MONSTERS

Frankenstein had the pipes of an angel
when chased by villagers, belting out
Christmas hymns in a sweet a cappella,
the dirges of the deity his jogging mix.
The Minotaur could whistle the ballads
of both man and beast with such aplomb
we did not heed the destruction of need,
the extinction of species deep in the maze.
The evil stepmother was hoarse and spent,
from repeating the same lullabies to send
wicked orphans from war into slumber,
a prince's kiss just the jolt of apocalypse.
The reality star king fidgeted on his throne,
a gold-plated toilet, belting out a battle
hymn of revenge, the unheard song bird
the most terrifying voice, staccato boots
as drums, acoustics of the echo chamber
creating an opera of one, a planet undone.

WOMAN FOUND WANDERING IN CALIFORNIA CLAIMS TO BE A MERMAID

Discovered without clothes and damp from a source
other than the sky, a woman with webbed feet
discusses the origin of her transformative state
with journalists and police. *In these days of borders
closing we are all mermaids*, she sang just before
ruminating about the sidewalk that was a river
and a river that was source of the internet.
We had long ago lost our ability to distinguish
truth or to extinguish fire that smoldered
from our exhaustion. Before long we saw
mermaids everywhere: riding rockets to overleveraged
real estate that even our president can't sell,
on milk cartons as the logo and the missing mythical
creature on back, or was that the venti tail on the grande
torso on the small coffee cup? The generals might
know or else it could be another ruse to hide
the cabal of foreign mermaids looking to keep
global warming a secret so the sea can be the arbiter
of life rather than the pool that reflects our nature.

Jaimes Palacio

FRANKENSTEIN & HIS BRIDE

I was born with broken signals buzzing
in my brain. God himself smiling
at the mess he made.

I had strange stories in my head calling
themselves dreams. I had an itch in my palms
for contact.

I wanted contact like a city wants tall buildings.
I wanted fire to engulf my stale
cardboard heart.

But nobody wanted my red eyes at the breakfast table.
My dent in their bed.

God found your pieces scattered. Put you together
for me. Your first reaction was to scream, and maybe
that crack I made: *What's up with your hair?*
wasn't exactly the wisest thing to say.

I wanted to love you, but you just wanted the violence.
Someone to slap your confused face. To make holes
in your pale trembling skin. To bury you quickly
in the past like the countless others Father once whispered to
under a dark and conniving moon.

HAUNTED

The German typewriter
years later would be equated
as hidden code to the Holocaust.
Shelly got sick. Started losing hair.
Rumors circulated: The elevator wouldn't emit
enough blood. The glucose kept shorting out
electric panels. Kubrick wanted the carpet to resemble
the moon landing some accused him of having a hand
in faking. The studio wanted Harrison Ford. Nicholson
was not King's choice. Preferred Christopher Reeve or Jon
Voight. The Timberline wasn't The Stanley. They requested
room numbers in the novel be altered. The twins
were not in the book. The twins were not twins. *All work
and no play* was filmed in various languages. Kubrick
could only think 42.42.42.

ROD SERLING IS NOT AN ARTICHOKE IN THE *TWILIGHT ZONE*

What we know is often sin, baby.
There are planes and trains to catch.
Bruises to hand out like business cards.

The sick man falls like a tornado.
Falls in love like friendly fire.
He misses you like bullets miss bodies.

The monsters are due on Elm Street
and they have pre-empted my favorite
program; the one that blinks and drops
time in its opening titles.

We are all vegetable or mineral in these
shallow ponds. This is just a toy-boat life
and that mountain is the face of a child
who has been spoiled beyond redemption.

That man in the dapper suit is not anything
ugly. The narrator of this story is not an artichoke.
An angry clock, or a bowl of bees.

He is not a pig nose they call beauty. He is not
an airplane running out of fuel over a prehistoric land.
Or a Talking Tina doll. He will not threaten to *kill you.*

The monsters are due on Elm street, but they are
running late. Did you not receive their text?
They will be arriving shortly. Please put out some nuts.

The sick man howls into the ocean. We are all vegetable
or mineral. He cries: *I am not!* The man in the dapper suit
is a reporter. The man in the dapper suit records seismic
disturbances. His cigarette is a baton to ward away monsters.

But monsters are due. They will arrive in a big, black
S.U.V. with Florida plates. They will have Telly Savalas's
severed head as a hood ornament. They will scream like televangelists.
They will ban gay marriage and burn all the sick, sick, twisted boys.

Alan Passman

IN MY TIME OF NEED, DRACULA COMES TO ME

The emerald mist slithers
under my doorway as he takes shape.
He's clad in black save
for the red velvet lining his cape.

His crimson eyes perch
over an aquiline nose,
not unlike my own,
which, underneath it, rests
a thin mustache. His alabaster
and ivory canines protrude
somewhat as he smiles
and bids me a good evening.

I don't bother to ask him why
he's come, and I do not fear him.
He, a regular fixture in my life
since childhood when I would dress
as him for fun, takes a seat at my bed's edge.

His thick, ebony hair slicked back shines
as if he and it were still alive. In a strong
but intelligible Romanian accent, he says:
My friend, what troubles you so that you might summon me?

On a conscious level, I didn't
and I don't know where to begin,
because while others might recede
from the darkness, I run
towards it full speed. There's safety
in the cover of night, in a darkened room,
and in thoughts on the lower end of mania.
Yet, I reply with one word, *Life.*

He says, *I have lived many years, and they pass*
like hours do for you and your kind. And I ask,
Why is there so much pain? His long-nailed hand
rests on my leg when he replies with the care
of a father, *That's how you know you're not dead.*

With head on hand, I ponder this musing
and tears well and pour and cover my cheeks
like a flash flood quenching a bone-dry riverbed.

And a single droplet of blood trickles from the corner
of one his eyes when he says, *My child, it would be*
my deepest hope to tell you that it gets easier, but I can't,
as I've had many a would-be hunter attempt to pierce
my heart with a wooden stake. Yet, here I am; I persist
through those that would help perpetuate my legend. Find
those people in your own existence, embrace them, and you
will live on forever through them." And I sit there, thinking

as the cruelest voice which lives inside and oft tries to usurp
the skull-sized kingdom of my mind screams from the recesses,
You will never find them! And it's as if this dark prince
of Wallachia hears and knows my thoughts, *A myriad of them*
are already here. Just gaze around, and you'll see who matters
and who believes you are important as well. And with that,

he becomes a bat, and I crack open my window, so he might fly
on to be someone else's villain, but right then, he was my hero.

THIS SHOULD BE READ IN THE VOICE OF VINCENT PRICE

Clawing up from the grave, the fingers of not dead,
but dormant memories sift and strafe their way through
the frigid loam of the back of my mind.

In them, there is darkness and light, sometimes dim
and sometimes bright. Who's to say what's wrong
or what's right? My own little *Fright Night*.

The bells toll above this cerebral cemetery
as all these undead corpses resurface. They move
with 1984-Michael Jackson's symmetry, swaying
and clapping in time with an unheard beat. I hear them
if no one else does, as I'm sure no one else does.

I scan the coffee shop from the stage where I'm reading
with mic in hand. All the audience sees is the living. I see
the deceased, because the skeletons in my closet have yet
to decompose, and remember, they're dancing to *Thriller*
in my head, taunting with asides and vagaries only I can
understand as they grumble and bark disgruntled.

And when in bed, clutching a pillow like a feature-less
Teddy Bear, I whisper to myself in a hoarse voice, *I don't
want to live anymore*, while Zapruder films of all my secrets
and transgressions play in a loop. I thought my wife was slumbering,
but she says with sleep in her voice, *That's not true*. She rolls
over to be my big spoon, and for a slight instant, the departed cease
they're shambling and gyrations. The death rattling of their chains
of torment become still, and the 90-mph carousel of my mind slows,
but doesn't stop. It never stops.

Steve Ramirez

THE VAMPIRE HOLDS OUT HIS OR HER HAND TO THE FISH MAN

as if it could help, as if it sold hope
from the convenience store of its unblinking eye.

As if one creature, so beautiful it transcends gender
could tiptoe to the opposite end of the genetic seesaw
and lift the fish man up with the weight of his or her gifts.

As if the mere promise could revoke the license to stare
granted to the entire town, the absolute mid-western casserole of them
with their leftover eyes, corn-fed lisps and the tractor pull whispers
which fuel a town with nothing left to learn.

As if the fish man's gills would become half-moon smiles on the landscape
of his neck or the black oceans of his eyes could remember
when girls thought they were the color of the sea.

Lee Rossi

CLOSE ENCOUNTERS OF ANOTHER KIND

F. now realizes that she should have paid closer attention in her exo-biology class.
At the time she didn't care that this particular species, whom she always thought of
    as "the Blob"
could fashion its pseudopodia into any form of appendage—head, or arms and legs,
her favorites being dorsal fins and the ridge of plates favored by Stegosaurus—
all quite convincing. No wonder they spread so quickly through the known planets,
these deft infiltrators, able to mimic the exact outlines of any apex predator.
What she was looking at was a fairly brawny male of her own species,
totally naked and sporting a giant penis, the size of a large flash light.
The fact that they were both floating in the zero gravity of her space ship
made the encounter almost laughable. Would her laughter have become alarm if she'd
    remembered
the creature's ability to simulate not just the form but the chemistry, in this instance
the sexual chemistry, of target species, chemistry which at the moment was causing her
to focus almost exclusively on the large red pseudo-glans aimed at her oral cavity.
After that particular docking maneuver, performed with more than the usual
enthusiasm, a certain recklessness even, they tried others, all of them
fairly pleasant—at least in her current state of chemically induced euphoria.
Give him credit, she thought, *he puts the X in extra-terrestrial.*
How she escaped the creature's ever-changing clutches, she couldn't remember.
Maybe he simply left. They do that. Maybe she blasted him into his constituent
molecules—she had done that, more than once—which in any case were now being
    filtered
from her air and water supply. All she knew was that one morning she awoke to find
her bed filled with a clutch of small needy creatures, which looked vaguely
like herself, only blobular. Oh well, she had always wanted to be a mother.
No reason to think her situation, floating out there all alone, would be any different
if the Blob had been human. Sometimes fake is just as good as the real thing.

Jennifer Lee Rossman

THE DOG WHO WALKED WITH ZOMBIES

The landscape was awash in death, a gray and dreary scene
that bordered on macabre at times and, other times, serene.

The life had gone from Earth and left its desiccated husk
to roam in perpetuity amid eternal dusk.

Humanity had crumbled as the dead began to rise;
survivors only ventured from their bunkers for supplies.

The hollow shells of people past, with lifeless eyes of black,
now wandered through the woods and towns, just waiting to attack.

They moaned and groaned and swayed their arms in listless, tired ways;
the hoards could stretch for miles and they walked for countless days.

Some smaller groups existed, made of half a dozen ghouls,
who likely once were families but now were vacant pools

where once had been a consciousness, where once existed dreams.
Their bodies were contorted into silent, endless screams.

They didn't know their families, and loved each other not;
they'd leave behind a fallen friend to decompose and rot.

Vicinity their only bond and food their only urge,
they wandered day and night to an imaginary dirge.

The dog who walked with such a group had loved her master so,
and by his side she faithfully had watched his spirit go.

And when he rose and walked again, she followed at his heel
and stayed with him as he went through his living dead ordeal.

He didn't smell the same, of course, and never scratched her head
the way he used to do each night before they went to bed.

He hadn't talked to her in months, emotions weren't shown,
and though the woods were full of sticks, they languished there, unthrown.

The loyalty she felt for him was not the least deterred,
and joyfully she trotted with her little zombie herd.

She left them periodically to go in search of food,
and here and there she caught some naps but never lost her brood.

Her very soul existed for her master, live or dead,
and moments when his hand would dangle low and touch her head.

For months - or maybe years - they walked, the zombies and the dog.
Around them swirled a smoky mist, an eerie, chilly fog.

They hadn't fed for quite some time. The dog was growing weak,
but now her nose detected it - the scent was quite unique.

She bounded forward recklessly, the zombies close behind.
To her the smell was ecstasy, a scent that did remind

of barbecues on summer days and sneaking table scraps,
and life before society had undergone collapse.

Her master had no memories, but he and all the rest
were guided by an instinct that could never be repressed.

They came upon a little house; the door was boarded shut,
and luscious smells of roasting beef came wafting from the hut.

A fence around the property prevented their advance,
and soon enough the zombies would recover from the trance

and shuffle off in search of something easier to eat.
The dog began to whine and bark, just longing for a treat.

The dog awaited eagerly, her tail began to thrash
from side to side and to the ground her drool began to splash.

The zombies that surrounded her were equally enthused,
and from their mouths and open wounds excitement slowly oozed.

A shot rang out, her master groaned and crumpled to the ground.
Another awful round of shots. Her zombies, all around,

were lifeless heaps of skin and bones. Her master wouldn't rise.
She licked his face and pawed his arm as sorrow filled her eyes.

Her mournful howls filled night and day. She never left his side,
and slept beside the rotting flesh of people who had died.

The person with the beef and gun attempted to persuade
the dog to come inside the house, but stubbornly, she stayed.

Her body slowly withered and her ribs did now protrude;
the life had left her soulless eyes, her growl was low and crude.

When she had nearly given up, her heart began to slow.
A light appeared before her eyes. Her master had to know

that she had been a loyal dog until the very end,
through life and death and life again, a zombie's faithful friend.

She closed her eyes and settled in, but then she heard a sound;
a little group of living dead was walking past the hound.

With nothing else to do but die, she found the strength to stand
and walked as one with all the dead that roamed across the land.

Beth Ruscio

CORRECTING FOR DEATH

I play this character
    Dead Judith on the call-sheet.
With a paint gun, a makeup specialist in effects
    sprays a dead person's face
        on my face.
Steady, with brushes made of a single eyelash,
hand mixed color concoctions are applied
    correcting for death.
Stria, for coagulation under the skin.
The mottled freckling of an overripe peach for blood splash.
A sculpted bullet hole in my temple.
An exit wound weeping syrup out my cheek.

Grips remove the rear-view mirror
from the 3/4-ton pick-up where I am slaughtered.
Not for my sake,
for the camera angle.
I'm in an onion field.
Gore drips off the shattered passenger side window.
Brains puddle on the Naugahyde seat.

Lunch isn't for hours:
we'll be on this shot forever.

Jason Schneiderman

LITTLE RED RIDING HOOD, SEASON 12

You'd think people would get tired of it
by now, the way the wolf dies at the end
of every season, but turns out not to have
died, and certainly, fans point out that the
Joker never dies in the *Batman* comics,
that Blofeld is always on his way back to
battle James Bond, and if anything,
the complaint that gains the most traction
is not that the Wolf should meet a singular
fate, like Circe or Moriarty (even though
he had his own tendency to come back),
but rather at how much more extreme
the peril that Little Red is placed in
each season. In season 8, the use of medieval
torture devices was extremely upsetting,
and several parenting organizations
boycotted the show after the suggestion
that Little Red had been experiencing
flashbacks in season 10, and that there
had been no wolf at all, only her fears and
trauma. I found season 11 the hardest
to take, and more or less stopped watching
after Little Red was doused in gasoline
and sobbing as the wolf flicked lit matches
at her and two corrupt cops in league
with the wolf explained to her how
they would cover it up. The bathtub scene
in Season 12 didn't entirely surprise me,
but still, that happened to someone
I know, and I won't be watching Season 13,
when they've promised to finally
kill the wolf and fill him full of stones,
because even if they keep their promise
there'll be another season as long as
there are still viewers, because
that's how stories work, how they keep
getting told, over and over and over,
as long as people will listen.

THE BUFFY SESTINA

The first episode of the new season, before the opening credits

Buffy is upstairs sharpening her large collection of stakes
when her mother comes upstairs and says, *Would it be bad,*
just this once, not to go out staking vampires again tonight?
After all—she had just defeated an apocalyptic force! Time
for a break? Buffy never has time for a break. Angel gone,
her stakes sharp, she kisses her mom and hops out the window

into the backyard. Buffy is familiar with this small window
at the beginning of every season (school year), when her stakes
are enough to fight her battles, and whatever the big coming
evil will be—it hasn't started to build yet. What big bad
will it be this season? She pulls her coat against the night
and there's Willow! Her best friend! She certainly has time

for Willow! They walk, explicate the summer, say, *Time*
to go back to school. Suddenly, a vampire seizes this window
of relaxed defenses, and grabs off-guard Willow. Oh, this night-
ly threat! Willow screams and resists. Buffy turns, her stake
at the ready. *Meet my friend, Mr. Pointy!* she says. Bad
bloodsucker, he lets Willow go. He wants to fight. He goes

at Buffy with everything, and Buffy (blue coat, boots) comes
back at him hard. The fight is oddly even. For a long time
(40 seconds, say), he gets in good blows. He hurts her bad,
she looks finished. She isn't getting back up again. A doe
leaps into the cemetery. All are distracted. Willow makes a stake
from a broken bench piece and the vampire tries to run into the night.

But Xander arrives, blocks the exit with his own stake. This night
is going terribly now (for the vampire)! The vampire goes
around to a crypt and tries to run inside, but it takes time
to pry open the gates. Too much time; Xander almost stakes
the vamp, but he stops to quip, and the effort goes bad.
The vampire throws him hard into the boarded-up window

of the crypt. Willow runs over, pulls a board from the window
for a new stake. Buffy's back up. Oh, what a luxury this night
is! Forever to fight just one, lone vampire. Xander's bad-
inage soundtracks the fight. Willow lunges and misses, coming
close, but too far left. Buffy kicks the vampire in face, stake
brandished. He goes down, and she's on top of him this time.

Buffy stakes the vampire. He's dust. Whew! Wait. Bad. Crypts
don't have windows. The night is heavy and dark. That took a long time!
What's coming begins to come. Let's unboard that window.

E.J. Schoenborn

IN WHICH I BECOME THE BABADOOK

I too hid in a closet for years,
wear hats every day,
make scrapbooks to be melodramatic,
and currently live in a basement.

When I am around,
mothers grab their children in fear
and ask, *What are you?*

I am a walking metaphor for mental illness.
I am all my anxiety dipped in oil
and set ablaze.
If you cloak my depression in a trench coat,
it is still there,
still depression.

When I look at food,
sometimes,
my mouth fills itself with glass,
a broken window
to let out the flies.

I peel back my skin
and cockroaches flood the kitchen.

My body is all the vermin
people want to exterminate.

Yesterday, I pretended I didn't exist.
And today, I wrote a book,
to remind the world
I do.

LIZ TAYLOR FROM *AMERICAN HORROR STORY* WALKS INTO A CAFÉ

I can feel them staring,
customers' eyes clinking together
like brandy snifters and whiskey glasses.

Almost like they've never seen a woman before,
or a goddess,
the way my hips scream from this black gauze
broad shoulders sequinned into purple scales:
Cut me and I bleed Dior.

At the register, the young pimply boy
tries to decide if he should say sir or ma'am.
Your Majesty works just fine, sweetie.

Black coffee, no cream, no sugar,
add Jameson from a flask
tucked into my ribcage.

I take a seat across the way from two girls
who whisper to each other and giggle--
my ears waterfall silver tinklings.
I hear *lady-man* and *girl-boy* and *freak*
curl my emerald fingernails
tighter around the cup,
chip the paint.

No pity party in my bar.
More whiskey.
Not in my bar.

THE DIFFERENCE BETWEEN A GHOST AND A SPIRIT, OR MY FAMILY IS MADE OF DEAD THINGS

A ghost tells you to get out of the house and never come back.
A spirit invites you in and offers you hot chocolate.

My sister doesn't remember her accident,
but maybe that's just the trauma
and all the blood spots on her brain.

A ghost comes in and slams all the doors when you're almost asleep.
A spirit carries you to your bed when you pass out during *Beauty and the Beast*.

Some days, when I talk to my mother,
her face becomes only a question mark.

A ghost shatters your favorite Winnie the Pooh bowl against the fireplace.
A spirit buys you a *Bugs Life* computer game for your 6th birthday.

My grandmother on my dad's side mixed up my sisters all Christmas.
"Lex looks different with glasses."
"Grandma, that's Saylor."

A ghost forgets to pick you up after track practice for the third time.
A spirit cheers from the sidelines as you run past.

I forget to take the hair out of the drain after I take a shower
again and again and again
and my memory is a winter lake filled with holes from ice fishing.

A ghost lives in a haunted house.
A spirit lives in a home.

Last week, I forgot my friend's name,
and just said, "Hey!" every time I saw them
until their body circled their way back into my skull.

A ghost is a shell of memory.
A spirit is a memory of a shell.
I wonder how many bodies I've forgotten.

A ghost lies down in your bed and sticks needles under your skin so you can't sleep.
A spirit whispers the sound of rain against the windows until your breathing slows.

My mother tells me she might be developing glaucoma.
She has become so much mother, her eyes might be filling with milk.
I am so scared my mother may never see me again,
that she will never see her child as anything other than a son,
a ghost.

The ghost in my body tells me my memories will haunt me forever.
The spirit says, *sometimes, it's better to forget, to just fade.*

Noel Sloboda

THE MUMMY AND THE PROM QUEEN

If he had just accepted he was a prop—
an older guy to lend her a sheen of cool—
he would not have bragged

about how he had bagged more
than his share of royal tail
back when he was so much

closer to god than man, before
being felled by an abscess, before
he eternally needed to be held

together by rolls of bandages.
He might have congratulated her
on winning a title, not worried

about whether she had more followers
online than he ever had in his temple.
But then he was cursed by Set,

so maybe nothing would have changed
her decision to run off before the last dance
with the second-string quarterback, leaving

the former pharaoh bereft as he crept
back to an empty sarcophagus,
sloshed from punch, half-unraveled

and chilled by night air, craving
the half-forgotten feeling of red-hot
sand between his toes.

THE SHRINKING GHOST

At first you said it was a trick of the moonlight. The ghost had been with us for a decade, since we first moved to Osgood Street. It belonged to our place. Yet now we both had to admit: the spirit was getting smaller. The funeral shroud went from king to twin. The faint smell of sulfur that once ushered the ghost into a room was gone. The nights grew tense—and long—as we worried about whether we could reverse the change. One evening, I left out an offering of cookies. The next you tried coins under pillows. Nothing helped. The ghost looked like a paper napkin tumbling in a breeze. Thinking it might need affirmation, we tried shrieking and trembling whenever we glimpsed the tiny specter. But the ghost continued to diminish. A few nights later, it was gone. Neither of us could stand it in that empty place. So, we booked a hotel room across town, paying for two months up front. When darkness falls, I sometimes talk about going back to Osgood Street, hoping the ghost might have returned. You want to believe it is still there, so miniscule it can't be seen by the naked eye. Every once in a while, you ask if things might have turned out differently if we had given the ghost a name.

Rob Sturma

SCREAM ON

it was the 90's / and we'd spent the decade previous getting hacked / as in machete hacked / and slashed / as in straight razor slashed / we were 80's babies / raised on sequels / where the horrors were men / who were not men / demons born of man / occupying woods / camps / cabins / boiler rooms / living rooms / chh chh chh / ahh ahh ahh / single note piano songs became warning anthems / we had sex and we died / we drank and we died / we smoked pot and we died / but somewhere in the middle of this frenzy / we became punchlines / death puns / we multiplied / like sequels / became formulas / rehashes / retreads / and it became time / to breathe new life / into our fears / so we deconstructed / made our fear into jokes / told our friends / how to survive through the night / we slathered on soundtracks / cast ourselves to look like our favorite teen stars / like that might help us live longer / but not really / we still ran upstairs / had unprotected sex to sarah mclachlan tunes / shotgunned beers / answered the phone / opened the door / patted ourselves on the back for making it / all the while knowing / that which does not kill us / will probably do so in the sequel

Richard Suplee

3AM BUFFY BINGE

after "When I am Dead My Dearest" by Christina Rossetti
& "Gutsongs" by Calvin Fantone

When I am undead, my dearest,

shove a branch through my chest,
my heart. Ignore my bloody mouth,

and my father's head in my left hand.
Shove a broken chair leg, a pool cue through

the unbeating muscle behind my ribs. Almost ash
already, please, my dearest, chop off my head

with a silver blade; use the dust, my dearest,
as mulch in your garden, as Miracle Gro.

Don't bury my skeleton. Smash it
with a sledgehammer in our garage. Repeatedly.

Throw me on the train tracks, the third rail
tie me to a stake. Dowse me in holy water, gasoline, oil,

latch a car battery to my nipples, enough volts to knock me out.
Keep it up all night, my darling.

When the sun rises, drop the match so I sparkle.

Ben Trigg

IT'S THE GREAT GREMLIN HUNT, CHARLIE BROWN

There are rules, Chuck.
You know that.
You were warned about water and food after midnight,
but the other kids were right when they called you a blockhead.
You thought it'd be easy.
Snoopy doesn't give you trouble so how hard could a new pet be?
I think Lucy's dying scream answered that question.
Now you have to make things right.
Gather Linus with his whip-like blanket and Patty with her home-run swing.
Go from home to home.
Save those lives you can.
Pray it doesn't rain.

Alexandra Umlas

AFTER READING THE *DOLLHOUSE MURDERS*

I ask my parents to take the dollhouse
and store it in the garage. In the book,
the dolls come to life, and the little girl wakes
each morning to the smallest figurines,
two inches of terror, in different rooms
than where she left them. One doll closes
the curtain of the kitchen window,
another poses, hand over stifled mouth,
sits on the couch, stares into air.

I couldn't close my eyes at night knowing
they didn't, even if they wanted to.
There was always a door, slightly open,
or a mark on the pink flowered wallpaper
that hadn't been there before.
Even after I covered the house with a quilt,
and slept with the light on, I could still hear
the brittle scratches of doll plastic against wood,
the baby crying from the yellow crib.

Reading brought those dolls to life: they
breathed and sighed and had to be laid
away in shoeboxes. That was the beginning.
Soon, there were siblings locked in our attic,
then a mad woman. Every dog had rabies,
each storm drain contained a clown. Books
hook their fingers into our eyes. We can't
help but open their covers, unshuttering
the crisp, white page—the indelible, dark ink.

ON THE FIRST NIGHT OF PASSOVER

I sit next to a woman at dinner who makes sounds
for the zombies on *The Walking Dead.*

Magenta beet-horseradish stains our lips, drips
onto porcelain. My daughter smears the juice

across her plate and I think of the Hebrew parents,
how their hands must have trembled as they applied

lamb's blood to their doorposts, how they must
have kissed their first-born sons before bed, how they

had to have thought *please let this work.* We dip
fingers in the wine, press down once for each plague,

and say them all, as if saying them will keep them
on the page. When we are done, our dishes are dotted

with crimson and I feel like making a zombie noise,
some guttural groan over the bitter herbs, dishes of tears,

shank bone, singing spun from our throats, haroset,
the crisp snap of matzo. *You know*, the woman whispers

over bites of brisket, *the zombies aren't the walking dead—*
and I realize exactly what that makes us.

TO MY HUSBAND

My mom won't take baths
when my dad is home. It's too risky:
the lavender bubbles, glass
of champagne, imagined footsteps
up the carpeted stairs, the door cracking
open, the hairdryer, which happens to be
sitting on the tile, plugged-in, slips
from his hands into the bath. The obituary...
an unfortunate accident— No one
would figure it after forty-nine years
of marriage, there would be no questions.
They've been this way for decades.

Me, a kid, only started to understand
when I saw *Sleeping with the Enemy*
for the first time. You know the one—
where Julia Roberts comes home
to perfectly lined-up bath towels,
cans stacked flawlessly in the kitchen.
When I visit other cities, when I happen
into a one-bedroom apartment, sparse
yet warm, with historic flourishes, a few
coffee cups in the cupboard, I think,
This is where I would like to live if
something happened to you.

Once, at the market, after we disagreed
on creamer and lunch meat, after I complained
of the heat and you shivered in the vegetable
section, after we carried the honey-crisp
apples in one of our reusable plastic bags,
as I loaded those bags into the trunk,
you had already climbed in, started
the engine; and I breathed in the car's fumes,
sure you were going to back over me.

Blame it on my parents.
Blame it on that movie, those perfect towels.
Blame it on the exhaust. Yes, the exhaust—

Charles Harper Webb

I MET THE HIDEOUS SUN DEMON

the summer I turned 8. My family
was visiting Aunt Ermyn in Chestertown—
founded 1706—a solemn, cemetery-
like place to a boy from Houston, Texas.

Every street was lined with iron gates
and oaks gnarled as witches' hands and full
of bats. Every house looked eons old,
and haunted. Aunt Ermyn's had dripping faucets,

creaky stairs, black wooden chairs where ghosts
and zombies rocked, and a grandfather clock
whose after-bedtime bonging sounded
like the footsteps of the Hideous Sun Demon,

a scaly giant who lived (I'm pretty sure)
in a volcano, leaping out to pitchfork people
through the heart, and eat them raw.
The instant he leapt, snarling, onto Chestertown's

one movie screen, he had me. Even though
I saw him fall into a lava-pool, he could
have swum out, or had brothers, hungry
for revenge. Every dark corner, parked car,

shadowy tree hid Sun Demons. My skin
burned, shrinking from those hypodermic tines.
I'd stall and beg and hold my bedtime off
past 9:00, but always end up shivering

in the top bunk of my cousin's bed, alone
except for Sam (12—sleeping like the dead),
and the Hideous Sun Demon who, I knew
from creaks and moans downstairs, was ransacking

the house for me. Only when I pictured
blue-eyed Candy Sanders in the Monster's
hands could I find the nerve to glare back
at his eyes red as lava-pools, and shower him

with rocks and Dad's most potent curses.
Every night he'd roar and hurl his pitchfork,
barely missing me, then lumber off with Candy
wriggling on his back, me on his heels,

until he tired and let her fall, and scrambled
up some high volcanic wall and disappeared
as sleep rolled in like fog, and running
toward me, smiling, sweet Candy saved me.

NIGHT OF THE LEPUS

The meteor
that hits his
hutches on
Palm Sunday
is so small,
the farmer
barely stirs
in bed. Next
morning, though,
farm and farmer are
gone: not eaten, burned,
or smothered in star-slime—
smashed to muddy ooze
by giant thumper-feet.
I forget how the crew-
cut hero (Poisoned
carrots? Crater Lake as a
stew pot?) kills the monsters.
I recall reaction shots: bearded Paul
Bunyans in skivvie-fouling fear, intercut
with snarling, buck-toothed, powderpuff-
tailed mutant bunnies. Ogled by a micro-
scope, the curviest blonde heroine looks
to support enough fanged jaws, tentacles,
and globs of goo to cast a million horror
shows. Science, like life, is scary stuff.
Yet true cuddliness exists. Some long ears
always bring a smile. Some fur seems
made to snuggle. Some eyes glow too
gently opaline to chill the scarediest kid's
spine. Some crinkly noses couldn't possibly
drag scaly Death behind. In this world, wild to kill
us all, some things are still too cute to be monsters.

ZOMBIE COTILLION

They can't remember dance steps
(did they ever know them?)
with their brains' brown slurry
sloshing in their heads. They keep

losing their partners—the boy-
dripping-maggots-from-his-eyes
groping for the gangrened girl,
her lipless mouth a jag-toothed

cave. It's clear as a torn-out
trachea, this is no fun. Hair
muddy as the grave, clothes
beyond the best dry cleaner's power

to save, they bump together,
stilled-heart-to-stilled-heart,
when all they crave is living flesh:
the screams, the crack of bone,

the arterial gush. They know
the company their misery seeks
quails behind barred doors, eager—
despite shotguns, fire, shovels

that bash dead faces into phlegm—
to cease their struggle
to get A's, make varsity, find
true love, master violin, see

their daughter marry an MD,
their son become one—to give up
life's losing battle, and join
them.

Ellen Webre

ADAMS, TENNESSEE
after the "Atlas of Cursed Places"

Surely there is nothing
so frightening
as an invisible woman
riding a dog with the head
of a rabbit. *Hut tut,*
what has happened now?
Yet another man gone
shock white at my banging
on the walls, at my devouring
of pillows and sheets, at my
present and intelligible love for
the lady of the house, who is
the most perfect woman alive.

My hatred echoes up from
the soil, oh how it plants
its poison in a body
just because I look at it.
I want him to die screaming,
and with belly full of rum,
I'll sing a drinking song
at the funeral. Call me Kate,
call me witch haunting,
I can throw you out the window,
faster than the British army.
Worship me in bluegrass
if you like, make me a star
of the silver screen,

but I will still burn you to
the ground if I feel like it.

TITHE TO HELL

The rubble pulses like a salt lamp,
    and I am a black-hatted girl
on a hillside, hands covered in bees,
    fingers dripping tongues
of amber and ash. I smear wax
    candles by thumb, I burn
the names of my deceivers, put forth
    amorous proposals to the moon.

My lips are stained with pomegranate,
    I draw the stars into my
palm. I carve the forests with their falling.
    Take their iron, my naked
sisters, build me a pyre in the snow.
    Let me lie upon it,
I am leaving this behind. My skin,
    my hair, my bones.

When the lady on the moon swallowed
    her elixir of immortal life
did it burn her from the inside? Did she
    dissolve into incense
like ghost money? Did it smell like
    honeysuckle? Is that
what drove her husband
    as mad for her as I am?

She sends her cicadas, her nightingale
    warbling at dawn and I know
it is time. I am stepping into the fire now.
    Will you ask me to stay?
Reach out your hand through the ritual
    for your little witch?
Take it, and I will pull you to me.
    I won't go without you.

Aruni Wijesinghe

ARRANGED BRIDEGROOM

pieced together from others'
misfortunes, you are a collection of wounds
ghost pain of missing limbs, lives you never knew

self-conscious of seams that refuse to heal
patchwork man, gaze into a stream
recoil from your own reflection

"alone bad, friend good"
the only love you know is a blind one
fraternity of the chronically lonely

wine and cheap cigars with the boys
collapse on the bed, stupefied
sleep off your ill-conceived bachelor party

steal from a victim of sudden death
unlike love, a human heart is
too complex to manufacture

the quickening of her
girl electrified
you love-struck, she stricken

wailing bride seeks refuge with
the awkward best man
Promethean matchmaker error

you get no say in the design of your mate
intrinsic disappointment of
an arranged marriage

CAMINANDO CON CALAVERAS
after Graciela Iturbide's "Procession, Chalma, Mexico, 1984"

Here in Chalma
death walks among us.
He is not a grim stranger
come to steal someone from town,
but more a beloved *tío*,
ever-present,
but still not to be entirely trusted.

We put on our masks of *papel maché*
that look like us, but not quite us.
We hope that *tío* will throw his arms about us
for a quick embrace,
but continue drunk-staggering up the street
to bother someone else.

Nancy Lynée Woo

KALI DANCES ON THE LONGEST DAY OF THE YEAR

She occurred on a cliff, scarf
red as venom, cradling
our sun in her arms. Streaks
of hair whipping upon
my shoulder—I was that close

to Kali. Extracted heart on palm,
I grew into her rage. Eight gold-
clanging arms struck the clouds
into mercy. I sobbed at her feet.
Blue sparks ravaging slick across

a finished empire, crack of thunder.
I called to my sisters, tried
to capture the goddess, keep her
breath on my neck & seize
my baby back at the same time.

But I couldn't stop her, couldn't
prevent the jagged fall of death.
I reached my arms out—
too late. The bundle fell, screeching
echo of a world in plummet.

She pulled me close, smiled wicked,
tender sighs opening, hands
waving upon the iris spreading.

LAMENT FOR A SKIN (ODE TO A SELKIE)

Salt flurry of wind rush
the boy running to his mother
    breathless—
this one moment agape forever.

Eyes like the crest of a wave
sea foam locks
heart stricken for the blue
    she sees what he holds.

Slick black skin, pelt shining
damp of seal—

she grabs it and the music plays.
    Doesn't even ask
where he found it,
kisses him tightly, yelling
for the others, sun-beaten arms
closing around them like a lid.

Quick, hard love and she
turns to release the door,
as blown about as
    the western wind.

Honey legs tumbling down
to shore, pillow of dress
sloughing off to sand,
    she catches
sight of a man, shadowy
in the distant green,
    stopping
as his fishing pole drops
toward a gallop.

But she is already at the sea
glistening joy of ocean mist
and her hands are already gone

and her legs are kicking into fin
and her lips are whiskering away
as the light plays upon the waves

and she calls to her children, goodbye.

Jonathan Yungkans

I'D LOVE TO COOK LIKE HANNIBAL LECTER

as I watch him caress a bunch of herbs—
dried a light, almost faded green—in both
hands, and release with a rub and contagious
grin their trapped oils. Herbs rain softly

onto fresh-ground kidney. Mixed, laid
gently in a hot skillet to sizzle, the dish
is food porn through a Chanel lens:
elegance you can taste with your eyes,

even if the meat, savored between sips
of a Château Montrose, is the uninvited,
the inquisitive, the rude. His closed eyes
and beatific smile shows how he adores

whom he eats. Maybe the Food Channel
could tap him for anger management,
culinary tips. The Travel Channel might
sign him to replace Anthony Bourdain:

another bad boy—a less wrinkled face,
fewer grey hairs in his manicured pate,
more Patagonia than T-shirt and jeans—
to stay a step ahead of law enforcement

while he treks through France, Morocco,
Vietnam and Venezuela, from rolling hills
to rain forest, and gets to know the locals
as he samples them in their native cuisines.

QUASIMODO—TO THE BANK AND BACK

Charles Laughton played me best. God,
he could act—his heart ripping

got yours, too. He was the man
in the moon, wished he were stone.

I love those lines. They made me
rich—a chateau and winery.

Hugo's book might be public
domain but my character's

copyrighted. Sure, I'd lose
Esmeralda—for a price.

Now, Disney—that mouse has fangs.
Ugly as me *and* lawyers.

Made me so close to "normal"
it was disgusting. Two eyes

instead of one. No deafness.
I sound like some cute puppy.

There was no me left of me—
just someone from Marketing.

Now there's a monster. Doubled
my acreage, though. Gargoyles—

especially corporate—
can be stone but have checkbooks.

Like Coppola said to me,
at least we have Cabernet.

SEVEN MONSTER THESES
after Jeffrey Jerome Cohen's article, "Monster Culture (Seven Theses)"

1. The monster's body is a cultural body.
(Weekends were my family hauling dog pens and multiple versions of Lassie to shows; weeknights varied from 19-cent hot dogs at Der Wienerschnitzel and five-dollar-carload movie Mondays at the Rodium Drive-In. The majority of kids at school were Japanese-American. They hated going to Japanese school on Saturdays, wanted to lounge instead of being force-fed katakana and heritage to the point of brain bloat. Their moms sent them to class parties with trays of sushi instead of *cupcakes*. None of the kids would talk to me directly.)

2. The monster always escapes.
(Late Saturday nights, blue-grey light flickered through the dark like pulses of a dream or random thoughts in a brain supposed to settle down for sleep. I was rooting for Boris Karloff as Frankenstein's monster, Lon Chaney Jr. as the Wolf Man. I could think of them instead of myself. Even so, I could feel all that extra hair sprout on my face and hands with the full moon. Wouldn't it be easier to open the steel clamps on my skull and pop in a new brain instead of doing homework? After all, I felt like Karloff as The Monster, head and shoulders taller than my classmates. Sometime in the movie, villagers with torches would gather, march through the night to dispatch them, and there I was back in class again.)

3. The monster is the harbinger of category crisis.
(The Wolf Man couldn't help but attack at least one person per film; the moon, his curse, and the Universal script writers drove him to it. I couldn't help but grow tall—with a shock of flame-red hair, to boot. By junior high, I was called "Towering Inferno" on a regular basis. I almost wished I could throw Irwin Allen into a basement, like The Monster did with that old biddie at the start of *Bride of Frankenstein* once he entered the picture, his skin blistered and crispy, his clothes probably reeking of creosote and burnt wood. Goddamned Irwin Allen. I felt every day like a walking disaster film. I wanted the full moon.)

4. *The monster dwells at the gates of difference.*
(Then there was Charles Laughton as Quasimodo in *The Hunchback of Notre Dame*—a film whose medieval streets, cathedral and town folk I swear I first saw in color, as though they lived and breathed right in front of me—even if the film was shot in black-and-white. When Quasimodo says his face is as shapeless as the man in the moon's, with his melting Camembert head and shoulder hump as massive as the upcoming school week, my tears don't trickle but flood—I know, inside and out, exactly what he means.)

5. *The monster polices the borders of the possible.*
(Boris Karloff, as The Monster, said, "We belong dead" at the end of *Bride of Frankenstein*; then his ham-sized hand pulled down a lever and he was reduced to atoms, at least until the next sequel. I thought he might have had a point, though I wished I could just dissolve into air, like Apollo in a *Star Trek* episode as he pleaded, toga-clad and laurel-browed, "Take me!" to the gods who had already departed. Apollo cried as he vanished.)

6. *Fear of the monster is really a kind of desire.*
(Lon Chaney Jr's face, in the Wolf Man films, twisted from the massiveness of Quasimodo's hump; I couldn't see the hump but could feel it, grinding both he and I like a pestle into dust. I saw Chaney as Lenny in the film *Of Mice and Men*, really just a huge child—another me. I couldn't stop crying at the movie's end, when George shot him. Why were people afraid of him? Why were people afraid of me?)

7. *The monster stands at the threshold of becoming.*
(Boris Karloff encased in sulfur—or was that Glenn Strange? The Monster was the Monster was the Monster. Lon Chaney Jr. was always the Wolf Man, except when he was the Monster, the Mummy, or Lenny. And Charles Laughton was always Quasimodo, even in *Spartacus* when he wore a toga and decided to disappear at the end of that film. The movies surrounding me and the TV set, me lying on the floor and Dad hopefully asleep in bed. I wish even now it were Saturday night.)

Mariano Zaro

FOURTEEN HORSES IN A SMALL CHAMBER

My father once told me
that fear waits piled up, like firewood,
outside the home of the heart.

It is your job to decide how much firewood
you want to bring inside.

Some people bring a single log,
a sliver, a shard, a splinter.

Some people carry armfuls of wood.
They stock up, they go back for seconds
as if invited to a feast.
Long-term fear almost undetectable,
sudden fear, soft fear
that feels like company or comfort.

Tonight, wild horses rustle
in the small chamber of the heart.
Unquiet hooves, lips twitching,
teeth clacking like clean stones.
They want me to open the door,
to let them out into the night
and the smooth uncertainty
of wet grass and fresh breeze.

Crickets are calling. Faint music
from a faraway town is calling.

I arrange the firewood inside,
each log like an old friend that
comes to remember the past.

I count the horses' heads. Fourteen.
It's time to lock the door.
We taste the security of roofs and walls.

So easy to obey the hand that obeys
the fear. So easy to light the fire.

ABOUT THE AUTHORS

Robin Steere Axworthy is a 4th generation California native who wandered off for many years before settling down in Southern California in 1983. She has been writing since childhood, but until recently only in the interstices of marriage, child rearing, teaching, dancing, reading, and historical reenactments, returning to seriously engage in writing after earning an MA from CSUF. She has been published in such places as *Cadence Collective, Incandescent Mind, Like a Girl*, and the anthology *Lullaby of Teeth* (Moon Tide Press). She takes joy in the variety of poems and poets in the local poetry community.

Devon Balwit lives scarily close to the Cascadia Subduction Zone. She has six chapbooks and three collections out in the world. Her individual poems can be found or are forthcoming in journals *The Cincinnati Review, apt, Posit, Cultural Weekly, Triggerfish, FifthWednesday, The Free State Review, Rattle*, etc. For more, see her website at: https://pelapdx.wixsite.com/devonbalwitpoet.

Laurel Ann Bogenis the author of 11 books of poetry and short fiction, including *Washing a Language, Fission,* and *The Last Girl in the Land of the Butterflies. Psychosis in the Produce Department: New and Selected Poems 1975-2015*was published by Red Hen Press in 2016. Since 1990, she has been an instructor of poetry and performance for the UCLA Extension Writers' Program. She is a recipient of the Pacificus Foundation's Curtis Zahn Poetry Prize and two awards from the Academy of American Poets. Her work has been translated into French, German, Italian, and Spanish, and has appeared in over 100 literary magazines and anthologies.

Amanda J. Bradley has published three poetry collections with NYQ Books: *Queen Kong,Oz at Night*, and *Hints and Allegations* and has published widely in literary magazines. A graduate of the M.F.A. program at The New School, Amanda holds a Ph.D from Washington University. She teaches at Keystone College outside of Scranton, Pennsylvania.

Derek D. Brown is an author, poet, and venture expressionist based in Los Angeles. His premiere collection of poems entitled *Articulate Scars: Comfortable Silences and Reluctant Tears,* was met with wide acclaim from poetry virgins and seasoned wordsmiths alike. His work was previously anthologized in *Voices from Leimert Park Redux: Los Angeles Poetry Anthology, Lummox #7,* as well as *These Pages Speak: A Youtube Creative Writing Course Reader* used by teachers to assist their students in the completion of college-level creative writing assignments. He's a highly coveted featured attraction throughout Southern California, whose mix of humor and truth in punchy poems has deeply embedded him in the fabric of the poetry scene.

Cathleen Calbert's writing has appeared in many publications, including *Ms. Magazine, The New Republic, The New York Times,* and The Paris Review. She is the author of four books of poetry: *Lessons in Space, Bad Judgment, Sleeping with a Famous Poet,* and *The Afflicted Girls.* Her awards include *The Nation* Discovery Award, a Pushcart Prize, the Sheila Motton Book Prize, and the Vernice Quebodeaux Poetry Prize for Women.

Michael Cantin is a poet and sloth fanatic residing somewhere in the wilds of Orange County, California. He writes fitfully between bouts of madness and periods of lucid concern. His poetry has appeared both online and in print. You can find his work in *The East Jasmine Review, Melancholy Hyperbole, 50 Haiku,* several anthologies, and elsewhere.

Adrian Ernesto Cepeda is the author of the poetry collection *Flashes & Verses... Becoming Attractions* from Unsolicited Press and the poetry chapbook *So Many Flowers, So Little Time* from Red Mare Press. His poetry has been featured in *Frontier Poetry, poetic diversity, The Wild Word, The Fem, Rigorous* and *Palette Poetry.* Adrian is an LA Poet who has a BA from the University of Texas at San Antonio and he is also a graduate of the MFA program at Antioch University in Los Angeles where he lives with his wife and their cat Woody Gold. Connect with Adrian at: www.adrianernestocepeda.com.

Sarah ChristianScher is a poet trapped in a biologist's body. She has been published in the anthologies *Like a Girl: Perspective on Feminine Identity,* published by Lucid Moose Lit and *Short Poems Ain't Got Nobody to Love,* published by For the Love of Words. She can be found most Wednesday nights at the *Two Idiots Peddling Poetry* weekly open mic. Sarah is supported in all this madness by a wonderful husband and a solid group of friends.

Nicole Connolly lives and works in Orange County, CA, which she promises is mostly unlike what you see on TV. She received her M.F.A. from Bowling Green State University, and her work has appeared, or is forthcoming, in such publications as *The Journal, Anomaly, Fugue,* and *Drunk in a Midnight Choir.*

Scott Noon Creley is the author *Digging a Hole to the* Moon (Spout Hill Press) and his work has been featured in the collections *Bear Flag Republic, One Night in Downey,* and *Cadence Collective: Year Two.* He is the founding chairman of San Gabriel Valley Literature Festival inc., a non-profit literacy foundation that holds monthly free writing workshops, monthly readings, and an annual community literature festival. He has an M.F.A. from California State University, Long Beach and lives with his wife, painter & photographer Carly McKean Creley, in Los Feliz.

Alexis Rhone Fancher is published in *Best American Poetry 2016, Verse Daily, Plume, Rattle,Diode, Pirene's Fountain, Cleaver, Tinderbox, Nashville Review,Wide Awake, Poets of Los Angeles, Duende, Hobart,*and elsewhere. She's the author of four poetry collections; *How I Lost My Virginity To Michael Cohen and other heart stab poems* (2014), *State of Grace: The Joshua Elegies* (2015), *Enter Here (2017),* and *Junkie Wife (2018).* Her photographs have been published worldwide, including the covers of *Witness* and *Pithead Chapel,* and a spread in *River Styx.* Alexis is a multiple Pushcart Prize and Best of the Net nominee, and is the poetry editor of *Cultural Weekly.* You can find her at www.alexisrhonefancher.com.

Brian Fanelli's most recent poetry collection is *Waiting for the Dead to Speak* (NYQ Books), winner of the 2017 Devil's Kitchen Poetry Prize. His writing has been published in *The Los Angeles Times, World Literature Today, The Paterson Literary Review, Horror Homeroom, Schuylkill Valley Journal, Main Street Rag,* and elsewhere. He has an M.F.A. from Wilkes University and a Ph.D. from SUNY Binghamton University. He is an Assistant Professor of English at Lackawanna College and blogs about horror movies and literature atwww.brianfanelli.com.

HanaLena Fennel, when asked about herself, says she "was born on a goat farm to a Jewish hippie; after that, things got weird." She is a proven champion of all things geek and credits the vibrant Southern California poetry community with helping her find her voice and always strives to support the voices of others. She works as an artist, poet, mentor, and can be found providing weekly prompts to an online community through her Patreon page: https://www.patreon.com/ HanaLenaFennel. Her first full-length collection of poetry, *Letters to the Leader: Poems Written in Response to the 55 Executive Orders from Donald J. Trump's First Year as President of the United States of America,* is forthcoming from Moon Tide Press in 2019.

Michael C. Ford's 2014 recording project titled *Look Each Other in the Ears* featured an elite cadre of Los Angeles musicians: not the least of which were surviving members of the notorious quartet most of you will remember as The Doors. His 2017 published volume is titled *Women under the Influence* and has forthcoming from Foothills Publishing in New York a 2018 fall title: *The War Chamber Ministry*. Also, in the late winter of 2018 Beyond Baroque, as part of their 50th anniversary, will market two chapbook-length poems in a doubleheader format with back-to-back Ford titles: *Manhattan Island Suite* and *Block Island Latitudes*.

Jerry Garcia is a poet, photographer and filmmaker from Los Angeles, California. His poetry has been widely published in journals and anthologies including: *Wide Awake: Poets of Los Angeles and Beyond (Pacific Coast Series), Coiled Serpent Anthology (Tia Chucha Press), Snorted the Moon and Doused the Sun: An Addiction Anthology, The Chiron Review, Askew Magazine,* and *The San Pedro River Review.* He has two books of poetry, the full-length collection *On Summer Solstice Road* (2016 Green Tara Press) and a chapbook *Hitchhiking with the Guilty* (2010 GND Press). Visit: www.gratefulnotdead.com.

Mike Gravagno is an amateur multi-hyphenate: a pop-culture critic, poet, nonfiction writer, copywriter, and podcaster. Mike received a B.A. in Creative Nonfiction from Columbia University, and an M.F.A. in Creative Writing from Chapman University, where he served as poetry/multimedia editor for the interdisciplinary graduate journal, *Anastamos*. Believing community is the key to everything, Mike hosts the reading/interview series *Writers Block Live!*and the drinking/reading series *Poetry on the Rocks*. His poetry, nonfiction, and reviews have been published in Columbia's *C.O.R.E.* blog, *Calliope, TAB, the Gordian Review* and the Moon Tide Press poetry anthology, *Lullaby of Teeth.*

Sonia Greenfield was born and raised in Peekskill, New York, and her chapbook *American Parable* won the 2017 Autumn House Press/Coal Hill Review prize. Her first full-length collection, *Boy with a Halo at the Farmer's Market*, won the 2014 Codhill Poetry Prize. Her work has appeared, or is forthcoming in the2010 and 12018 Best American Poetry, *Antioch Review, Bellevue Literary Review, Los Angeles Review, Massachusetts Review,* and *Willow Springs.* Her collection of prose poems *Let down* is forthcoming in 2020 from White Pine Press as part of the Marie Alexander Series. She lives with her husband, son, and two rescue dogs in Hollywood where she edits the *Rise Up Review* and co-directs the Southern California Poetry Festival.

Seth Halbeisen has escaped from the great state of Ohio, and has been described as a cunning combination of amazingly helpful and frighteningly annoying. Seth enjoys shiny objects, selected chocolates and cheeses, and the stringing together of complicated words. If seen in public, please do not throw food at him; it excites him. Seth has been published in *Horror-Ku* by *Freeze Ray Poetry*, and in multiple anthologies by Raundi K. Moore-Kondo and published by For the Love of Words.

LeAnne Hunt (she/her) grew up in the Midwest and now lives in Orange County, California. She is a regular at the Two Idiots Peddling Poetry reading at the Ugly Mug in Orange and at the Poetry Lab workshop in Long Beach. She has poems published in *Black Napkin Press*, *Lullaby of Teeth: An Anthology of Southern California Poets* and *Incandescent Mind*, Winter 2017. She publishes a blog of writing prompts at www.leannehunt.com.

Born in Beirut, Lebanon, **Arminé Iknadossian** immigrated to the United States in 1974 to escape the civil war. She is the author of *All That Wasted Fruit* forthcoming from Main Street Rag Press. She earned an M.F.A. from Antioch University where she was awarded a fellowship from *Summer Poetry in Idyllwild*. After teaching English for 20 years, Iknadossian wrote *United States of Love & Other Poems* (2015). During her tenure as a teacher, The Los Angeles Writing Project awarded Iknadossian a fellowship for their summer residency. Iknadossian currently lives close to the sea with Henry the Cat. Find out more at armineiknadossian.com.

Victor D. Infante is the Entertainment Editor for *the Worcester Telegram & Gazette*, the editor-in-chief of *Radius* and the author of *City of Insomnia* from Write Bloody Publishing. His poems and stories have appeared in dozens of periodicals, including *The Chiron Review*, *The Collagist*, *Barrelhouse*, *Pearl*, *Spillway*, *The Nervous Break down* and *Word Riot*, as well as in anthologies such as *Poetry Slam: The Competitive Art of Performance Poetry*, *Spoken Word Revolution Redux*, *The Last American Valentine: Poems to Seduce and Destroy*, *Aim For the Head: An Anthology of Zombie Poetry*, *The Incredible Sestina Anthology* and all three *MurderInk: Tales of New England Newsroom Crime* anthologies. He ain't afraid of no ghost.

Jeanette Kelly is a Southern California mixed media artist with a love of horror films. She returned to writing after reconnecting to her poetry roots two and a half years ago in a local poetry workshop. Both her poetry and art focus on communication and connectivity. Recently she co-produced *Bridges*, a multimedia exhibit and performance of 39 original works by composers, artists and poets.

Ron Koertge, a fixture in the L.A. poetry scene for decades, writes fiction for young adults and poetry for everybody. His most recent book of poems is *Olympusville*, a hybrid from Red Hen Press marrying poetry/illustration. A skillful handicapper of thoroughbred race horses, he can be found most afternoons at Santa Anita Race Track. That's him in the hat.

Elmast Kozloyan is a poet trapped in limbo between magic and reality (though seldom chooses the latter). At the age of fifteen won the silver medal for poetry in the Scholastic Art and Writing Awards and since then has released her debut chapbook, *Doe Eyed Venus*, and is published in such places as *Cadence Collective*, *Poetry in Motion*, *Pacific Review*, the *East Jasmine Review* and *The Los Angeles Times*.

Pat M.Kuras was a Pushcart nominee in 2017. She has long been a horror fan. Her poems have appeared in *Crab Creek Review*, *Nerve Cowboy*, *Prison Renaissance*, *Ramingo's Porch* and *Writing in a Woman's Voice*. She has two chapbooks: *Hope: Newfound Clarity* (2015) and *Insomniac Bliss* (2017), both from IWA Publishing Services.

Zachary Locklin is the author of *My Beard Supports Nothing: The Facebook Poems* from the Weekly Weird Monthly Press. A graduate of the University of Southern California›s Master's of Professional Writing program, he now teaches composition, creative writing, and literature at California State University, Long Beach.

Los Angeles poet **Rick Lupert** created the Poetry Super Highway (poetrysuperhighway.com) and hosted the Cobalt Cafe weekly reading for almost 21 years. He's authored 22 collections of poetry, most recently *Beautiful Mistakes* and *God Wrestler: A Poem for Every Torah Portion* and edited the anthologies *A Poet's Siddur*, *Ekphrastia Gone Wild*, *A Poet's Haggadah*, and *The Night Goes on All Night*. He writes the Jewish Poetry Blog *from the Lupertverse* for www.JewishJournal.com, and the daily web comic *Cat and Banana* with fellow Los Angeles poet Brendan Constantine. He's widely published and reads his poetry wherever they let him.

Tony Magistrale is a professor at the University of Vermont, where he teaches courses on horror film, the gothic, and a class that fills up in seven minutes called *Hollywood's Stephen King*. He is also the author of the book by the same name, which is the first academic study of movies adapted from the King canon.

Jennifer Martelli is the author of *My Tarantella* (forthcoming, Bordighera Press), as well as the chapbook, *After Bird* (Grey Book Press, 2017). Her work has appeared or will appear in *The Sycamore Review*, *Sugar House*, *Superstition Review*, *Thrush*, and *Tinderbox Poetry Journal*. She has been nominated for Pushcart and Best of the Net Prizes and is the recipient of the Massachusetts Cultural Council Grant in Poetry. She is a poetry editor for *The Mom Egg*.

Lincoln McElwee holds a Bachelor's and Master's degree in English Literature from California State University, Fullerton. He's also studied poetry, opera, and fiction in both Italy and Ireland. He loves traveling and wine and books and wine. His influences include W.H. Auden, Ezra Pound and James Joyce. He currently works as a freelance writer/editor in Los Angeles, California.

Daniel McGinn is the author of *The Moon, My Lover, My Mother & The Dog* (Moon Tide Press, 2018) and *1000 Black Umbrellas* (Write Bloody, 2011). He is a native of Southern California who's led writing workshops at Half Off Books, The Orange County Rescue Mission, charter schools and poetry venues. Daniel received his M.F.A. in writing from Vermont College of Fine Arts. Daniel has been married to the poet and painter, Lori McGinn, for 41 years.

Ally McGregor is an M.F.A. student of Poetry at California State University, Long Beach. She is a Southern California native and currently resides in Long Beach. She can frequently be found studying Surrealist literature, drinking copious amounts of coffee, and binge-watching horror films.

Carrie McKay is a poet and teller of tall-tales. A convert to the So Cal weather, she began writing as a child in Cleveland during those many rainy days. She can often be found reading and listening at the *Two Idiots Peddling Poetry* reading in Orange County. Her most recent publications can be found in *The Silver Birch Press: Mythic Poetry Series*, *Defenestration*, *A Poet is a Poet No Matter How Tall: Episode II Attack of the Poems* and *Beyond the Pillars: An Anthology of Pagan Fantasy*.

Ryan McMasters is an internationally published performance poet out of Pasadena, Texas. He is the author of three books of poetry: *Polarize*, *Co. Lab Oration*, and *Connect the Dots*. McMasters can be seen via the *Write About Now's* YouTube Channel. His latest work is published in Dublin, Ireland's *HCE Review*, and he has poems forthcoming in *Peculiar Journal*. Find him twittering & instagramming @rmcmastewriter.

José Enrique Medina earned his B.A. in English from Cornell University. He writes poems, short stories, and novels. His work has appeared in *The Burnside Review, Reed Magazine, American Writers Review*, and other publications. When he is not writing, he likes playing with his bunnies, piglets and baby chicks on his farm.

R.S. Mengert has an M.F.A. in poetry from Syracuse University. He lives in Tempe, Arizona and teaches Creative Writing at Phoenix College. His poems have appeared in *Poetry is Dead, Zymbol, Maintenant, Four Chambers, Enizagam, The San Pedro River Review, Fjords, ABZ Poetry Magazine, The Café Review*, and *Snail Mail Review*.

Ryan Meyer is a Connecticut poet who recently published a collection of horror poetry called *Haunt*. His work has appeared in *Freshwater Poetry Magazine, The Beechwood Review*, and in his alma mater Southern Connecticut State University's *Folio Literary Magazine*. He currently works in Globe Pequot's marketing department, handling titles for Falcon Guides, the premier publisher of outdoor recreation and adventure titles. Ryan posts updates on his work at www.NothingPeak.com.

Bill Mohr is a professor in the Department of English at California State University, Long Beach, where he has taught literature and creative writing since 2006. His most recent book is a bilingual volume of poems, *The Headwaters of Nirvana / Los Manantiales del Nirvana*, published by What Books/Glass Table Collective. His literary history of L.A. poetry, *Holdouts*, was published by the University of Iowa Press in 2011. In addition to Spanish, his writing has been translated into Croatian, Italian, and Japanese. He blogs atbillmohrpoet.com; his website iskoankinship.com.

Eric Morago is a Pushcart Prize nominated poet who believes performance carries as much importance on the page as it does off. He is the author of two poetry collections: *What We Ache For* (Moon Tide Press, 2010) and *Feasting on Sky* (Paper Plane Pilots, 2016). Currently Eric hosts a monthly reading series, teaches writing workshops, and, as of 2017, is the new editor-in-chief and publisher of Moon Tide Press. He has an M.F.A. in Creative Writing from California State University, Long Beach, and lives in Los Angeles, CA.

Eileen Murphy lives near Tampa with her husband and three dogs. She teaches literature/English at Polk State College in Lakeland. Her poetry has been widely published in literary journals including, recently, *Rogue Agent, Tinderbox Journal* (nominated for Pushcart Prize), *Thirteen Myna Birds, Writing in A Woman's Voice, Whale Road, Sonic Boom, Rag Queen,* and a number of others. She's also a staff writer for *Cultural Weekly* magazine. Her website is mishmurphy.com.

Ashley Naftule is a writer & theatre artist from Phoenix, AZ. He's been published in *Vice, Ghost City Press, The Hard Times, Phoenix New Times, Occulum, Pitchfork, L'Ephemere Review, Bandcamp, Mojave Heart, Rinky Dink Press, Coffin Bell, Amethyst Review, Four Chambers Press, Spiral Nature, Popula, Hypnopomp, The Molotov Cocktail,* and *Ellipsis.* He's a resident playwright and Associate Artistic Director at Space55 theatre.

Robbi Nester is the author of three books of poetry: a chapbook, Balance (White Violet, 2012) and two collections, *A Likely Story* (Moon Tide, 2014) and *Other-Wise (Kelsay, 2017).* Her new book, *Narrow Bridge,* is forthcoming from Main Street Rag.

Martina Reisz Newberry's most recent books are *Never Completely Awake* (Deerbrook Editions, 2017) and *Take the Long Way Home* (Unsolicited Press, 2017). She is the author of *Where it Goes* (Deerbrook Editions), *Learning by Rote* (Deerbrook Editions), and *Running Like a Woman with Her Hair on Fire: Collected Poems* (Red Hen Press). She has been widely published in literary magazines in the U.S. and abroad. Passionate in her love for Los Angeles and for her husband, Brian Newberry (a Media Creative), Martina lives there with him.

Terri Niccum is a backyard birder who enjoys jabbering with mockingbirds. Her chapbook, *Looking Snow in the Eye,* was released in 2015 by Finishing Line Press. Her poems have appeared in *Cadence Collective* and in the *Incandescent Mind* anthologies *Volume 2* and *Selfish Work.* Her work has also been featured in *The Poeming Pigeon* anthologies *From the Garden* and *Love Poems, Nimrod International Journal, The Maine Review, 1932 Quarterly Review, Literary Orphans, Angel City Review,* and *Pretty Owl Poetry.*

Andrew November came from the future to change the outcome of World War II. Thanks to him, Hitler is dead, and the middle of the week is now called Wednesday (you're welcome, btw) But his time machine ran out of fuel and now he's stuck here. Andrew has decided to stay to help preserve the punk rock scene and its pivotal role in the defeat of the upcoming alien invasion of 2046. Andrew has recently stopped drinking for good, and now only drinks for evil. You can find more of his haikus and other writings atwww.uptowndrunkpunk.com.

Martin Ott has published eight books of poetry and fiction, most recently *Lessons in Camouflage* (C&R Press, 2018). His first two poetry collections won the De Novo and Sandeen Prizes. His work has appeared in more than two hundred magazines and fifteen anthologies.

Jaimes Palacio has written for periodicals, hosted/booked award-winning readings such as *Penguins Hooked on Macronics* and has appeared in many forms of media, including *Radius, A Poet is a Poet no Matter How Tall, Attack of the Poems!, A Poet's Haggadah* (even though he is not Jewish!) and, most recently, *Snorted the Moon & Doused the Sun*. Kristen Stewart once liked his poems.

Alan Passman has been published by and in *Crack the Spine, Carnival, Bank Heavy Press, East Jasmine Review, Cadence Collective, Silver Birch Press*, and featured in *Multiverse: An Anthology of Superhero Poetry of Superhuman Proportions* from Write Bloody Publishing. He received his B.A. and M.F.A. from California State University, Long Beach for Creative Writing and Poetry respectively. Currently, he teaches English at Long Beach City College. He has a soft spot for superheroes, Horror, and root beer.

Steve Ramirez hosts the weekly reading series, *Two Idiots Peddling Poetry*. A former member of the Laguna Beach Slam Team, he's also a former organizer of the Orange County Poetry Festival, a former member of the Five Penny Poets in Huntington Beach, and current full-time nemesis of Eric Morago. Publication credits include *Pearl, The Comstock Review, Crate, Aim for the Head* (a zombie anthology) and *MultiVerse* (a superhero anthology).

Lee Rossi is a freelance poet living in Northern California. His poems, reviews, and interviews have appeared widely in venues ranging from Poetry Northwest to the Southeast Review. He is a paragon of modesty.

Jennifer Lee Rossman is a science fiction writer and sometimes-poet who would survive the zombie apocalypse in a tricked-out wheelchair. Her work has been featured in several anthologies and her time travel novella *Anachronism* is now available from Kristell Ink, an imprint of Grimbold Books. She blogs atjenniferleerossman.blogspot.com and tweets @JenLRossman.

Beth Ruscio is a poet, daughter of actors, an accomplished actress herself (*The Unicorn, Dreamland, 28 Days, View From the Bridge*), mentor (Otis College of Art and Design), nominee (Pushcart Prize), finalist (The Wilder Prize, Two Sylvias Prize, Sunken Garden Poetry Prize, Tupelo Quarterly Prize, Ruth Stone Poetry Prize), published (*California Journal of Poetics, Cultural Weekly, Tupelo Quarterly, Spillway, In Posse, Malpais Review,* speechlessthemagazine), anthologized (*Beyond the Lyric Moment, Conducting a Life: Maria Irene Fornes, Poet's Calendar, 1001 Nights*). Her poem "Correcting for Death" is a slightly fictionalized account of playing dead in the movie *Letters from a Killer*.

Jason Schneiderman is the author of three books of poems: *Primary Source*(Red Hen Press 2016),*Striking Surface*(Ashland Poetry Press 2010), and *Sublimation Point*(Four Way Books 2004). He edited the anthology *Queer: A Reader for Writers* (Oxford University Press 2016). His poetry and essays have appeared in numerous journals and anthologies, including*American Poetry Review, The Best American Poetry, Poetry London, Grand Street,* and The Penguin Book of the Sonnet.An Associate Professor of English at the Borough of Manhattan Community College, CUNY, he lives in Brooklyn with his husband Michael Broder. His next book of poems, *Hold Me Tight*, will be out from Red Hen in 2020.

E.J. Schoenborn [they/them/their] is a white, nonbinary trans femme spoken word poet and rural trans-plant from Wisconsin living in St. Paul, Minnesota. Most of their written work touches on the intersection of (trans)gender & queer identity, mental illness, working class & rural life, rape/sexual assault as a survivor, and opossums. Their poetry has been published in *Freeze Ray Poetry, Runestone Literary Journal, Rising Phoenix Review, The Holy Shit Journal, Voicemail Poems, Button Poetry*, and more.

Noel Sloboda is the author of the poetry collections *Shell Games* (sunny outside, 2008) and *Our Rarer Monsters* (sunnyoutside, 2013) as well as several chapbooks, most recently *Risk Management Studies* (Katty wompus, 2015). He has also published a book about Edith Wharton and Gertrude Stein. Sloboda teaches at Penn State York.

Rob Sturma is the editor of the zombie-themed anthology Aim for The Head (Write Bloody Publishing) and the editor-in-chief of the pop culture lit journal *FreezeRay.* His favorite scary movie is the original *Nightmare on Elm Street* but his favorite horror icon is Jason Voorhees. In another lifetime, he drank with Spike from *Buffy The Vampire Slayer.* He resides in Oklahoma City but vacations in Parts Unknown.

Richard Alexander Suplee is a poet from Philadelphia. He completed his Master's in Fine Arts in Creative Writing at the University of San Francisco where he lived for three years. His poems appeared in *Spiral Poetry Zine* and *Hyphen.* He has written articles on poetry for *Switchback* and about comic books, movies, and anything nerdy for Phawker.com.

Ben Trigg is the co-host of *Two Idiots Peddling Poetry* at the Ugly Mug in Orange, California. His full-length collection *Kindness from a Dark God* came out on Moon Tide Press in 2007. He co-edited the anthology *Don't Blame the Ugly Mug: 10 Years of 2 Idiots Peddling Poetry* published by Tebot Bach. When all else fails, Ben goes to Disneyland.

Alexandra Umlas is from Long Beach, CA and currently lives in Huntington Beach with her husband and two daughters. She has an M.F.A. in Poetry from California State University, Long Beach and an M. Ed. in Education with an emphasis in Cross-Cultural Teaching. You can find her work in *Rattle, Rise Up Review, Poets Reading the News, Cultural Weekly, Mothers Always Write, Lipstick Party Magazine, indicia, F(r)iction, The Poet's Billow, Modern Loss, Rip Rap* and elsewhere, or at alexandraumlas.com.

Charles Harper Webb's latest collection of poems, *Sidebend World,* was published by the University of Pittsburgh Press in 2018. *A Million MFAs Are Not Enough*, a gathering of Webb's essays on contemporary American poetry, was published in 2016 by Red Hen Press. Recipient of grants from the Whiting and Guggenheim foundations, Webb teaches Creative Writing at California State University, Long Beach.

Ellen Webre is a multicultural poet and life-long learner. She is the social media specialist for Moon Tide Press and the Two Idiots Peddling Poetry Reading in Orange, CA. She is currently working towards a Master's in Teaching at UCI, and has a B.A. in screenwriting at Chapman University. Her poetry largely explores the celestial and supernatural, myth and folklore. She has been published by *Voicemail Poems, Vanilla Sex Magazine, Gingerbread House Lit, Black Napkin Press* and The *Metaworker.*

Aruni Wijesinghe works as a project manager for Affinis Labs, an award-winning social innovation firm that helps clients creatively tackle complex global challenges through entrepreneurship. She holds a B.A. in English Literature from UCLA, an A.A. in Dance from Cypress College and is certified to teach English to Speakers of Other Languages (TESOL). Aruni has read her poetry at Angels Flight Literary West salons, Roar Shack reading series and Poetry Circus 2018. She lives a quiet life in Orange County with her husband Jeff and their cats Jack and Josie.

Nancy Lynée Woo is a PEN Center USA Emerging Voices Fellow, a co-founder of the Long Beach Literary Arts Center, and the author of two chapbooks, *Bearing the Juice of It All* (Finishing Line Press, 2016) and *Rampant* (Sadie Girl Press, 2014). She teaches poetry workshops in Long Beach called *Surprise the Line*. You can find her online at nancylyneewoo.com and support her work at patreon.com/fancifulnance.

Jonathan Yungkans remains a fan of classic Universal horror films, the TV series *Hannibal* and Cabernet Sauvignon. An M.F.A. Poetry candidate at California State University, Long Beach, he is aided by copious amounts of coffee and swears his blood type must be French Roast. His work has appeared in *Lime Hawk, Twisted Vine Literary Journal, West Texas Literary Review* and other publications. His poetry chapbook, *Colors the Thorns Draw*, was released by Desert Willow Press in August 2018.

Mariano Zaro is the author of four bilingual books of poetry. His poems are included in anthologies and literary journals in USA, Mexico and Spain. He has translated American poets Philomene Long, Tony Barnstone and Sholeh Wolpé. His narrative received the 2004 *Roanoke Review* Short Fiction Prize and the 2018 *Martha's Vineyard Institute of Creative Writing* Fiction Prize. Zaro hosts a series of video-interviews with prominent poets as part of the project Poetry.LA. (www. Poetry.LA). Since 2016, he has served as a trustee of Beyond Baroque Literary Center (Venice, CA). He is a professor of Spanish at Rio Hondo College (CA).

ABOUT THE ARTISTS

Tyler Kinnaman is the owner and manager of Trigger Happy Tattoo and has been tattooing professionally for fifteen years. He mentored under Dave Brewer, who is now his partner. Tyler has also been a successful muralist and has done graphic design work for the past fifteen years for such bands as Subline with Rome, Dirty Heads, Offspring, and Pepper. He loves all forms of art and looks forward to learning something new every day.

Leslie White is an artist, jewelry designer and maker, and a jack of all trades as far as DYI is concerned. She has done everything from illustrating books to professionally designing and building escape rooms. Leslie has a true passion for all things horror and sci-fi, while still loving all things sweet and adorable. This mix gives her artistic style an interesting and individualistic combination of humor, gore, and heart all at once. She lives in San Juan Capistrano, California, where she runs her online jewelry shop. You can find her jewelry work on Instagram @ fogandhowl and email art commission inquires to artbylesliemwhite@gmail.com.

ACKNOWLEDGEMENTS

Moon Tide Press and the poets in this anthology are grateful to the following publications where these poems have previously appeared, sometimes in a different form:

"After Watching David Lynch Movies" — *Chiron Review*

"Afternoon with Redón"— *Boy with a Halo at the Farmer's Market* (Codhill Press, 2015)

"Also Frankenstein" — *Psychosis in the Produce Department: New and Selected Poems, 1975-2015* (Red Hen Press, 2016)

"Bones Dig this Dream" — *Psychosis in the Produce Department: New and Selected Poems, 1975-2015* (Red Hen Press, 2016)

"Cagey" — *Word/For Word*

"Dear Dracula" — *Geography of the Forehead* (University of Arkansas Press, 2000)

"Everyone Knows a Wolf Can't Smile." — *The Moon, My Lover, My Mother, & the Dog* (Moon Tide Press, 2018)

"Faith Healer" — *Digging a Hole to the Moon* (Spout Hill Press, 2014)

"For Sale: Baby Shoes, Never Worn" — *Sidereal Magazine*

"Haikus by Jason Vorhees" — *FreezeRay Poetry Horror-Ku Special*

"I Met the Hideous Sun Demon" — *The Panhandler*

"In Which I Become the Babadook" — *FreezeRay Poetry*

"Lament for a Skin (Ode to a Selkie)" — *San Gabriel Poetry Quarterly*

"Milk Carton Kids" — *LUMINA*

"Mrs. Victor Frankenstein" — *Vampire Planet* (Red Hen Press, 2016)

"Mutation" — *American Writers Review* "Night of the Lepus" — *The Burnside Review*

"Niños de la Tierra" — *The Burnside Review* "October Knob and Broom" — *Psychosis in the ProduceDepartment: New and Selected Poems, 1975-2015* (Red Hen Press, 2016)

"Queen Kong" — *Queen Kong* (NYQ Books, 2017)

"Rod Serling is not an Artichoke in the Twilight Zone" — *Radius*

"Self-Portrait as First Slut to Die in a Horror Movie" — *Drunk in a Midnight Choir*

"The Abominable Snowman" — *Fever* (Red Hen Press, 2006)

"The Buffy Sestina" — *Primary Source* (Red Hen Press, 2016)

"The Ghoul Convention" — *Skidrow Penthouse*

"The Oldest Rules in the Book" — *Haunt* (Ryan Meyer, 2018)

"The Sacrifice" — *The Plath Poetry Project*

"The Shrinking Ghost" — *Quarter After Eight*

"Tlaltecutli by Starlight in Puerto Escondido" — *Willawaw Journal Poetry & Art*

"Villain" — *Queen Kong* (NYQ Books, 2017)

"We Provide for Ourselves Our Own Horror" — *The Demented Chauffeur and other Mysteries* (Ion Drive Publishing, 2009)

"Werewolf, 2000" — *Geography of the Forehead* (University of Arkansas Press, 2000)

"Womb" — *Post Mortem*

"Women and Children First" — *Los Angeles Review*

"You're a Good Zombie, Charlie Brown" — *Feasting on Sky* (Paper Plane Pilots, 2016)

THE LAST SCENE BEFORE THE CREDITS ROLL, AFTER THE MONSTER IS BELIEVED DEAD, BUT COMES BACK FOR ONE FINAL SCARE (OR A PARTING NOTE OF THANKS FROM THE PUBLISHER)

From the moment Michael Miller (thank you Michael Miller!) passed Moon Tide Press over to me, I had envisioned this anthology. I knew others would share my interest—I just didn't know how many. I was floored by the number of submissions we received. I want to thank everyone who submitted to this project, and of course, to all those whose poems appear in this book. I feel good about what we are unleashing unto this world (I sound like a mad scientist there, don't I?) and know I couldn't have done it without you. I am grateful for your voices and for entrusting Moon Tide with your words. I especially want to share my gratitude for a number of folks that contributed a little something extra to seeing this collection come alive. Thank you Ray and Christi Lacoste, Zachary and Tammy Locklin, Terri Niccum, Andrew November, Jeanette Kelly, José Enrique Medina—you know what you did. I especially want to thank Leslie White and Tyler Kinnaman for their amazing art, Michael Wada for his design work, and Ellen Webre for her marketing and social media finesse. I would also like to give thanks to the following venues that have supported Moon Tide Press in the past and continue to do so: The Whittier Museum (huge thank you for hosting the launch for this book), The Whittier Art Gallery, Half Off Books, and 1888 Center. Next, I want to share my appreciation for all of Moon Tide's past authors, future authors, and subscribers and patrons; you help keep this Press alive (It's alive! It's aliveeeeee!). Thank you. I'd be remiss if I didn't thank my wife, Katie O'Shaughnessy, who listens to and supports me on this crazy journey of bringing other people's poetry into the world—even if that poetry might be about ghosts, zombies, and vampires. Lastly, I want to thank you, dear reader, for picking up this book—I hope you found it as enjoyable as it was for me when I was putting it together. Like the pieces of some creature, I was just waiting on the electrical charge of lightning to bring it to life. You are my lightning. Thank you for your jolt.

PATRONS

Moon Tide Press would like to thank the following people for their support in helping publish the finest poetry from the Southern California region. To sign up as a patron, visit www.moontidepress.com or send an email to publisher@moontidepress.com.

Anonymous
Robin Axworthy
Conner Brenner
Bill Cushing
Susan Davis
Peggy Dobreer
Dennis Gowans
Half Off Books
Jim & Vicky Hoggatt
Ron Koertge & Bianca Richards
Ray & Christi Lacoste
Zachary & Tammy Locklin
Lincoln McElwee
David McIntire
José Enrique Medina
Andrew November
Michael Miller & Rachanee Srisavasdi
Terri Niccum
Ronny & Richard Morago
Jennifer Smith
Andrew Turner
Mariano Zaro

ALSO AVAILABLE FROM MOON TIDE PRESS

Drop and Dazzle, Peggy Dobreer (2018)
Junkie Wife, Alexis Rhone Fancher (2018)
The Moon, My Lover, My Mother, & the Dog, Daniel McGinn (2018)
Lullaby of Teeth: An Anthology of Southern California Poetry (2017)
Angels in Seven, Michael Miller (2016)
A Likely Story, Robbi Nester (2014)
Embers on the Stairs, Ruth Bavetta (2014)
The Green of Sunset, John Brantingham (2013)
The Savagery of Bone, Timothy Matthew Perez (2013)
The Silence of Doorways, Sharon Venezio (2013)
Cosmos: An Anthology of Southern California Poetry (2012)
Straws and Shadows, Irena Praitis (2012)
In the Lake of Your Bones, Peggy Dobreer (2012)
I Was Building Up to Something, Susan Davis (2011)
Hopeless Cases, Michael Kramer (2011)
One World, Gail Newman (2011)
What We Ache For, Eric Morago (2010)
Now and Then, Lee Mallory (2009)
Pop Art: An Anthology of Southern California Poetry (2010)
In the Heaven of Never Before, Carine Topal (2008)
A Wild Region, Kate Buckley (2008)
Carving in Bone: An Anthology of Orange County Poetry (2007)
Kindness from a Dark God, Ben Trigg (2007)
A Thin Strands of Lights, Ricki Mandeville (2006)
Sleepyhead Assassins, Mindy Nettifee (2006)
Tide Pools: An Anthology of Orange County Poetry (2006)
Lost American Nights: Lyrics & Poems, Michael Ubaldini (2006)

Made in the USA
Middletown, DE
19 June 2022

67397862R00106